Norah McMeeking

BELLA BELLA
Sampler Quilts

9 Projects with Unique Sets ◆ Inspired by Italian Marblework ◆ Full-Size Paper-Piecing Patterns

C&T PUBLISHING

Text and Lifestyle Photography copyright © 2013 by Norah McMeeking

Photography and Artwork copyright © 2013 by C&T Publishing, Inc.

Publisher: Amy Marson

Creative Director: Gailen Runge

Art Director: Kristy Zacharias

Editor: Liz Aneloski

Technical Editors: Sadhana Wray and Alison M. Schmidt

Cover Designer: April Mostek

Book Designer: Rose Wright

Production Coordinator: Jenny Davis

Production Editor: Alice Mace Nakanishi

Illustrators: Norah McMeeking and Wendy Mathson

Photo Assistant: Mary Peyton Peppo

Flat Quilt and How-To Photography by Christina Carty-Francis and Diane Pedersen of C&T Publishing, Inc., unless otherwise noted; Lifestyle Photography by Norah McMeeking, unless otherwise noted

Published by C&T Publishing, Inc., P.O. Box 1456, Lafayette, CA 94549

Library of Congress Cataloging-in-Publication Data

McMeeking, Norah, 1949-

  Bella bella sampler quilts : 9 projects with unique sets - inspired by Italian marblework - full-size paper-piecing patterns / Norah McMeeking.

    pages cm

  ISBN 978-1-60705-641-6 (soft cover)

1. Patchwork--Patterns. 2. Quilting--Patterns. 3. Cosmati work. I. Title.

  TT835.M472 2013

  746.46--dc23

                            2012042244

Printed in China

10 9 8 7 6 5 4 3 2 1

DEDICATION

For Elinor Rose and any cousins she may someday acquire, and to all those who sent me photos of their "bella bella quilts" (you made my days!)

THANKS SO MUCH TO ...

All of those who kindly asked me when I was going to write another book

C&T's amazingly dedicated people, from the front desk to the shipping room;
Liz, Kirstie, Sadhana, Rose, Diane, Ruthmary, Jenny, and Alice

The Bella Brigade: Barbara Aspen, Mary Ballard, Isabel Bartholome, Irelle Beatie,
Julie Cohen, Karin Cooper, Ky Easton, Jan Inouye, Colby Kline, Adela LaBand,
Jean Morrison Phillips, and Sandy Wilmot

Hoffman California–International Fabrics

Michael Miller Fabrics LLC

Northcott Silk Inc.

Timeless Treasures Fabrics of SoHo LLC

Aurifil USA

CM Designs Inc.

Olfa–North America, division of World Kitchen LLC

Longarm quilters: Dee Angus of Tomorrow's Treasures, Kim Peterson of
Kimberwood Quilting, and Paula Rostkowski of A Quilter's Work

Professor Roberta Massabo, University of Genoa, for translations and geometry terms

Dianne Trower, for helping me keep it together

Ann McGill, for double-checking

And my husband, Bob, for making me cups of tea that I let go cold beside
the sewing machine; for running out for more magenta ink for my printer so
I could stay in my pj's and type; and last of all, for leaving me alone so
I could "get on with it!" You're my darrrrling.

CONTENTS

Author's Note 5

A Brief History of the Designs 6

How to Get the Most from This Book 8

Why Use Paper Foundation Piecing? 10

Choosing Fabric 12

Glossary 15

General Instructions 17

Quilt Projects

Project 1: Ciao Bella! 28

Project 2: Viterbo 34

Project 3: Laterano Interlace 40

Project 4: Salerno Sampler 45

Project 5: Portico Pavement 53

Project 6: Orvieto Sampler 60

Project 7: San Clemente Borders 70

Project 8: Sicily Souvenir 78

Project 9: Diamante Delight 86

About the Author 95

Resources 95

AUTHOR'S NOTE

I'm a lover of puzzles and patterns. On a long-anticipated trip to Venice, where I first set eyes on the marble floors of St. Mark's Basilica, I discovered these interests meshed fabulously with quiltmaking. At the time, making a "floor quilt" seemed daunting, but after I cut my quiltmaking teeth, I realized foundation piecing was a great way to achieve the wow factor that had so impressed me in Italy.

I've been thrilled to hear from readers of my first book, *Bella Bella Quilts*, that other quilters, too, have been inspired by these age-old designs. And I have been even more thrilled to see photos of their quilts (some with ribbons!) based on the Bella patterns.

After writing *Bella Bella Quilts*, I was fortunate to return to Italy, visiting Rome and later Sicily, to see more floors. Sure enough, I found even *more* to inspire me, and so this new book commenced. I hope you'll enjoy it and will send me pictures of *your* finished masterpieces!

—Norah

Photo by Anne McMeeking

The Cosmati is the collective name of a group of designers active in Italy during the Middle Ages. They repurposed stone elements from the ruins of imperial Rome to pave cathedral floors and decorate buildings and monuments. Massive pillars were sliced into disks, giving rise to distinctive curvilinear designs. The sheer number of stone pieces lends power to the simple shapes employed in the floor patterns. The texture, variety, and color of the marble make a strong link to patchwork.

The designs in *Bella Bella Sampler Quilts* are derived from patterns found in medieval churches throughout Italy and would look familiar to any of the Cosmati that might come by your sewing room.

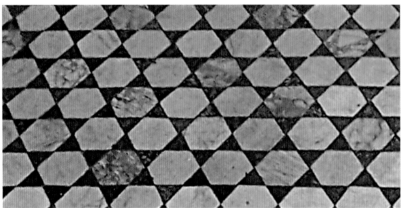

Floors typically use Carrara marble mixed with green, gold, and dark red stone.

Gold leaf on glass

Orvieto Cathedral facade

Palatine Chapel, Palermo, Sicily

READ THE GENERAL INSTRUCTIONS, PLEASE!

I know quilters hate to read directions, but General Instructions (pages 17–27) includes some good ideas and techniques you might not have come across. I *promise* you'll save time, and perhaps even aggravation, if you'll just take the time to read them. The tips scattered within the project instructions are useful in many circumstances as well. So settle down with a nice cappuccino and get inspired!

MIX AND MATCH

By all means, copy the sample quilts if you wish, but the goal here is to make it "mix-and-match simple" to make a unique version of the master quilts. Choose a project and note its "ingredients." For example, a design might require 4 sections that finish 12″ × 12″, 4 sections that finish 24″ × 12″, and a section that's 24″ × 24″, as shown in the diagram (next page). The 12″ × 12″ section could be made of 16 blocks 3″ × 3″ or 9 blocks 4″ × 4″ or 4 blocks 6″ × 6″. The rectangular section could, in a similar manner, consist of 32 blocks 3″ × 3″ or 8 blocks 6″ × 6″, and so on. The 24″ × 24″ center could be similarly varied.

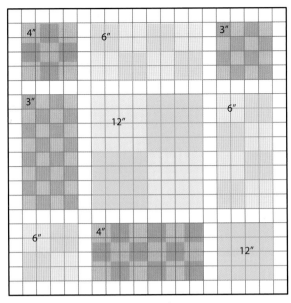

Underlying grid is of 3" squares.

ENDLESS DESIGN POSSIBILITIES

- Substitute whole pieces of fabric for some of the pieced units. A beautiful print that coordinates with the patchwork can substitute for an entire section of blocks.

- Use plain fabric in place of patchwork to show off your hand- or machine-quilting skills.

- Achieve a more formal effect by using the same block pattern in all the units.

- Use compasses or medallions in the center square.

- Use a different selection of blocks or change the color palette.

- Substitute beautiful appliqué for all or part of the patchwork.

ote

If foundation piecing is not your cup of tea, measure the master diagrams on the pattern pullout sheets to determine finished sizes of the patches. Add seam allowances and piece traditionally.

WHY USE PAPER FOUNDATION PIECING?

- *It is very, very accurate!*

- *All* the precision is on the foundation, so you don't have to rely on your rotary cutting accuracy or the machining of your presser foot width to get perfect matches—just sew on the lines.

- Paper foundations allow you to work with shapes that require Y-seams, or with tiny pieces, or with sizes that aren't marked on the ruler—for example, $1^{11}/_{16}$" or those nasty three-decimal-point diagonal measurements.

- *Nothing* works better when you're piecing bias edges.

PAPER FOUNDATION PIECING
THE WAY I DO IT

Paper foundation piecing is easier to *do* than to think about, so you'll have to *try* it, not just read about it. Think of it as learning a new quilting method and allow yourself a learning curve. Like anything, techniques and methods can vary. Here's what, I think, sets *my* methods apart:

There are no seam allowances on the foundation patterns, so …

- You don't have to remove tiny ¼" shreds from the seam allowances later.

- It's easy to get hold of the foundation to remove it.

- If you don't *see* fabric around the edge of the foundation, you're more likely to notice there's a problem.

- The edge of the foundation is a stitching guide. Sew right beside it.

- Measure against the edge of the foundation when you trim (see Foundation Piecing Process, page 20).

All the patches are cut generously oversized before you begin, so remember …

- Precut all the foundation patches, because it can really drive you crazy when the patch doesn't cover the space required. Those angles are tricky! Preshaping helps get you in the ballpark before you start to sew. Add about ½" seam allowance as you cut.

- Though this book has measurements, foundation patches don't have to be perfect. If you make a little slip, don't throw that patch away—it will probably still work.

- The big, shaggy margins that accumulate around the foundation give you more to hold on to when you pin units or blocks together. Plus, they make it easier to press the seams open without burning your fingers!

Leave the foundation papers in until the bitter end because they …

- Stabilize bias edges.

- Sometimes have tick marks to help you join sections accurately.

- Make the blocks and units lie nice and flat.

- Help you see mistakes in the joining seams (essentially, the stitches are on the paper!).

- Serve as labels and help you keep patches organized.

THE *DISADVANTAGES* OF PAPER FOUNDATION PIECING

- **Everything is backward.** There's this reversing thing with paper foundation piecing. The foundations have lines, which you look at, sew on, and often think of as "the front." Most times, that's fine—unless the block is asymmetric or directional. After it's sewn, if you look at the *fabric*, the Flying Geese that were headed east when you were looking at the foundation will be flying west. This characteristic can lead to confusion—so if something looks wrong to you, turn it over and look again.

- **You have no choice** about which direction a seam lies, but you can grade your seams. If need be, you can trim sections and remove the paper before joining units. This allows you to re-press some seams in the opposite direction to allow more seams to marry. When push comes to shove, press seams open to distribute bulk.

- **It uses a bit more fabric** than traditional piecing, but it is so accurate! Besides, using up fabric is good.

CHOOSING FABRIC

Above: Theme fabric with supporting fabrics of green, purple, and gold

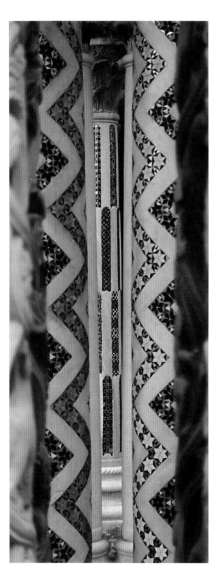

These designs are based on marble floors whose coloration is quite varied. Part of what makes them so exciting is that every fragment of stone is a little different from every other one. Nothing really matches, and that characteristic takes away much of the stress of fabric selection. If you have a quilter's stash of fabrics or remnants, gather some coordinating fabrics and get started.

I like to fill a storage tub with fabric, both large and small pieces. I keep an eye out for a couple of yards suitable for bands. Sewing unit by unit, I try out what I think looks good. It's like cooking. Now and then I add a little spice by finding a color that echoes a tiny detail in a print—the color that's the *least* obvious in the print. I choose the setting and background fabrics last, like the side dishes in a meal. For those, I often choose fabrics that are not included in the piecing. I avoid prints that will compete with the patchwork for the viewer's attention. Those beauties I save for dessert!

WORKING WITH YOUR STASH TO MAKE A FABRIC PALETTE

Choose a theme fabric or a combination of two or three colors, such as green, purple, and gold, as a starting point. Sort through your stash and add coordinating fabrics, being sure to select *dark, medium, and light values*. Keep print texture in mind and vary it to add interest. Keep choosing until you have more fabric than you think you'll use.

The more varied the colors and values, the easier it will be to use the palette in a great assortment of blocks. Save large scraps and trimmings for "emergencies" until the project is completed.

WORKING WITH A PURCHASED MEDLEY

If you need a starting point, it's fun to work with a medley of fat quarters. Many shops and catalogs feature these, and choosing one is a bit like being in the penny-candy store! Purchase duplicate bundles if necessary. You can stretch the assortment by adding coordinating fabrics from your stash.

Choose medleys with a full range of dark to light.

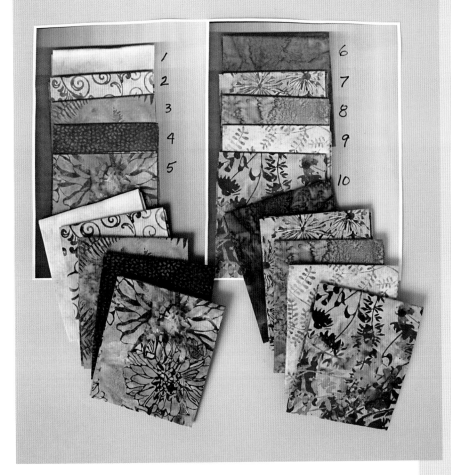

Tip

After you've chosen a palette of fabrics, a fat-quarter medley for example, fan out the fabrics and make a color copy. Label each fabric on the copy.

Work with the fabrics to decide the placement within the blocks and note the chosen fabric on the block diagrams. This allows you to design before you cut up any fabric. If you think you don't have enough of a special fabric, calculate how much you need beforehand.

COMMERCIAL PRINTS AND SOLIDS

Don't restrict choices for these quilts to only batiks or designed-as-stone fabrics. Who says you're making a floor? Use what you love—roses, paisleys, designer prints. In addition, certain designs with light, narrow lines against a background (tree branches, lace, grass) often resemble marble when cut into small pieces. Directional fabrics are great fun. Be sure to mix in solids and "blenders" to allow the eye to rest. Buy fat quarters or fat eighths of solid-reading fabrics available in a range of colors, such as Krystal or Fairy Frost by Michael Miller Fabrics or Marbles by Patrick Lose by Moda, to add to the prints you already have. Northcott's Stonehenge line has a huge selection of both theme and blender prints.

Some print fabrics can resemble stone when cut up.

Tip

The fabrics at left show both color and value selection and the relative strength of solids. Solid fabrics tend to stand out among the prints, so if you use them, be sure to include several in different colors and values. Mix them throughout the design for sparkle.

GLOSSARY

GEOMETRY TERMS

 60° diamond
Diamond with four equal sides and opposite angles of 60° and 120°

Arc
Any section of a circle

Diagonal
Line from corner to corner of a square or rectangle

 Equilateral triangle / 60° triangle
Triangle with three equal sides, each coming together at 60°; half of a 60° diamond

Half-circle
One-half of a circle

 Hexagon
A shape with six sides. Hexagons in the quilts in this book have six equal sides.

Isosceles triangle
Triangle with two equal sides and two equal angles

Obtuse angle
An angle greater than 90° but less than 180°

Right angle
90° angle

Square sides
Sides of any shape that come together at right angles

SEWING TERMS

Add seam allowance as you cut.
Use a ruler to measure ¼″ from the template or foundation edges to add the seam allowance when you trim a piece. Foundations for blocks do not include seam allowances; however, templates indicated by **T** in the cutting charts include the seam allowance.

Block
Composed patchwork unit

Cutting size
Measurement that patches should be cut; includes seam allowance

Cutting template
Author's term for a roughly traced freezer-paper template used to cut patches that are awkward to cut with a rotary cutter. *Seam allowances of ½″ need to be added on all sides of the cutting template.*

Dot
A point where two seams will cross when sewing is complete

Filler blocks
Partial blocks used to complete a row or unit

Finished size
Measurement of a patch or block, from the front of the patchwork, after all sewing is completed

Foundation
Pattern, usually of paper, used for sequential piecing

Grade the seam
Cut the seam allowances in graduated widths to reduce bulk. Grading can help keep dark fabrics from showing through on the right side of a quilt.

Half-square triangle

Triangle made by cutting a square patch on the diagonal, in one direction, from corner to corner to make two triangles. Both square sides will lie on the straight grain of the fabric.

Marry seams

When joining patches and blocks, position seams so they meet in opposing directions, allowing the small steps created by the seam allowances to lock snugly and accurately together.

Partial seam

Technique in which part of a seam is sewn and other pieces are joined before the first seam is completed. It is useful for adding borders that wrap around corners and for avoiding Y-seams.

Patch

An intentionally cut piece of fabric that is part of a block

Pin matching

The use of a single pin at the exact point of a seam match; anchor pins are inserted on each side of the match pin, which is then removed.

Quarter-square triangle

Triangle that is made by cutting a square patch into four pieces, cutting from corner to corner on both diagonals. The square sides of each triangle will lie on the bias.

Reverse or _r_ label on a template or patch

Indicates a patch that is a mirror image of a corresponding patch

Rows

Blocks or sections sewn side by side to each other

Scrappy

Made with a random or haphazard mixture of cotton prints and solids

Section

Part of a block that must be added to another part or parts to make a complete block

Template

A carefully made shape of paper or plastic that is used to cut an unusual shape accurately

Tick mark

A line or arrowhead on the pattern used for matching seams

Units

Rows or arrangements of blocks that complete a component of a quilt design

Value

The relative darkness or lightness of a fabric when compared with other fabrics

WOF

Width of fabric, usually between 40″ and 44″

CUTTING PATCHES

Rotary Cutting Common Shapes

Most patches can be cut with a rotary cutter. Most of us cut squares, rectangles, and half- and quarter-square triangles all the time. The cutting charts in the projects use a little symbol for each.

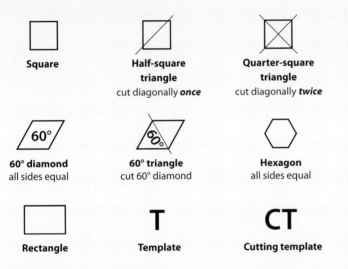

Square

Half-square triangle
cut diagonally *once*

Quarter-square triangle
cut diagonally *twice*

60° diamond
all sides equal

60° triangle
cut 60° diamond

Hexagon
all sides equal

Rectangle

T
Template

CT
Cutting template

All sizes listed in the charts are cutting sizes.

Cutting Other Shapes

Diamonds are less commonly cut, so here's a review on how to use strips and a rotary cutter to make 60° diamonds and, from those, to make 60° triangles and hexagons.

DIAMONDS

Cut diamonds from strips. The width of the strips is specified in the text. The 60° lines on a quilter's ruler can be used to cut a 60° diamond.

The width of the strip is the constant measurement (4˝ in the example).

- Find the 60° angle line on the ruler. Rulers vary—some are right-handed only, some have angles on both edges—so take care to find the 60° angle.

- Place the angle line on the ruler along the side of the strip and trim off the end of the strip. Whether the angle goes up or down doesn't matter.

- Rotate the strip and position its side on the angle line again.

- Keeping the angle line on the edge of the strip and the ruler on top of the strip, line up the cut edge with the grid on the ruler. Slide the ruler so the distance from the angled cut to the edge of the ruler is *the width of the strip* (4˝ in the example).

- Double-check the alignment and angle and cut the strip. Under the ruler you'll have an equal-sided 60° diamond.

- For more diamonds, reposition the ruler and cut, keeping the distance between cut edges the same as the strip width.

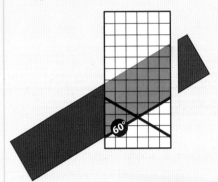

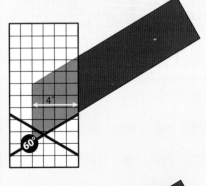

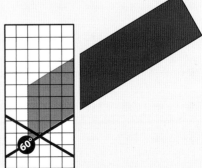

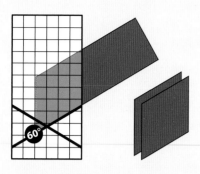

CUTTING DIAMONDS IN HALF TO MAKE TRIANGLES

Cut 60° diamonds in half (the short direction) to create 60° triangles—equilateral triangles with 3 equal sides and 3 equal angles.

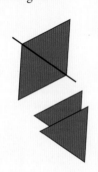

HEXAGONS

Hexagons are cut from 60° diamonds.

- Cut a strip the required width (4", shown by the yellow arrow).

- Cut a 60° diamond from the strip.

- Take half the width of the strip (2" in this case) and measure that distance from the obtuse angles of the diamond to the cutting edge of the ruler. Align the obtuse angles with the measurement line. Trim off the triangle that extends.

- Rotate the patch and line up the side you just cut with the line for the width of the strip (4" in the example). You should notice the angles lining up again on the halfway line too.

- Trim off the extending triangle, and there will be a hexagon under the ruler.

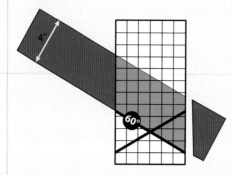

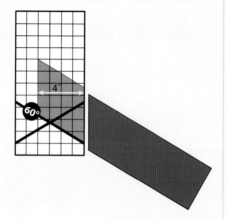

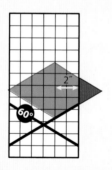

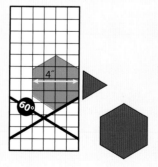

USING CUTTING TEMPLATES

Very unusual shapes, such as kites, are easiest to cut if you use a cutting template. Patches that need a cutting template will be indicated by **CT** in the project cutting charts.

> ### Note
>
> For foundation piecing, cutting templates do not have to be perfect tracings. Remember, there will be extra seam allowance added around them, so don't waste a lot of time drawing them perfectly. No one will ever know!

1. Trace the patch specified from its master pattern onto the dull side of freezer paper. If you need a lot of patches, trace several templates. Stack fabric in layers so you can cut many patches at once.

2. Iron the cutting template to the *wrong side* of the fabric. This is important—especially with asymmetric shapes!

3. Space the cutting templates an inch or more apart so there's a gap between them for the seam allowances. Use a quilter's ruler to check the spacing if you don't trust your eyes. Keep patches on grain when possible.

4. Cut down the middle of the gap, ½″ from all the sides of the cutting templates, to make oversized patches.

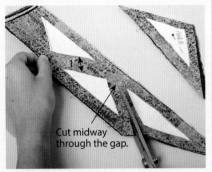

Cut midway through the gap.

Layer strips, wrong sides up; press cutting templates to the top layer; and cut down the middle of each gap.

MAKING FOUNDATIONS

Master patterns for all the foundations are on the pattern pullout sheets. Duplicate them accurately. It is often helpful to label foundations for color placement, print direction, and so on. Be sure to write with something that won't smear, run, or iron onto the fabric, such as the true black Faber-Castell Quilter's Pen (by C&T Publishing).

Foundation Paper

There are various specialty quilting foundation papers on the market, including Quilter's Freezer Paper Sheets for inkjet copiers and Carol Doak's Foundation Paper (both by C&T Publishing). Uncoated sandwich wrapping tissue (available in restaurant supply stores) also works well and is easy to remove, but it is quite fragile. Freezer paper from the grocery store can be used, but only by tracing, not with a copier.

Copying

If you photocopy foundations, make sure the copier does not distort them. When you're sewing 25 pieces together, a ¹⁄₁₆″ mistake turns into a 1½″ mistake. Most copiers can be adjusted, both horizontally and vertically, if required. Test by drawing a perfect square on a piece of plain paper, making a copy, and measuring the copy carefully; then adjust the copier settings if need be.

Check that the copy doesn't smear or transfer toner or ink when ironed. If this happens, careful use of a pressing cloth will keep the toner off the fabric. You just don't want to find out the hard way that the toner smears!

Tracing

Tape tracing paper or freezer paper over the master diagram. Use a thin, flat ruler and a very sharp pencil to carefully trace the lines. Work with good lighting. The time you spend doing this will be rewarded with accurate blocks.

Making Needle-Pierced Duplicates

Once you have a good copy or tracing, use it on top of a layer of several sheets of foundation paper. Staple the stack together (the more staples, the better) inside of and outside of, but not *on*, the lines. Unthread your sewing machine, put in an old needle, and "sew" carefully on the lines. This procedure perforates the stack, making lines of holes where the traced lines were.

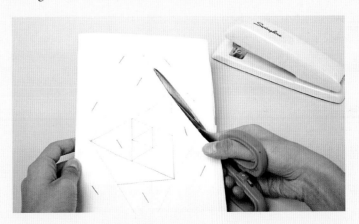

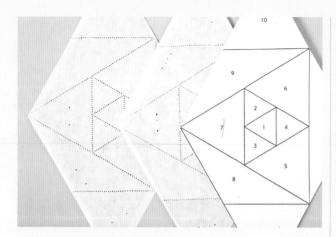

Note

When tick marks (small arrowheads) appear on the foundation, they indicate where a seam from a different section touches that foundation. Some foundations have tick marks where you might want to use a seam in a variation of the block or set.

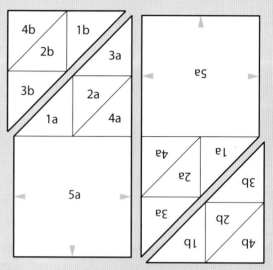

Anatomy of a foundation: Numbers indicate piecing order of patches, and letters indicate sections. Foundations can be copied and rotated to create blocks.

Tip

It is unnecessary to needle pierce the outline of the foundation. Just cut that line to transfer it through the stack.

Before layering and stitching, test to see how many layers of paper your sewing machine can handle without laboring. Test also to determine which stitch length produces a good line without causing the foundation paper to separate.

MASTER FOUNDATION PATTERNS

The master foundation patterns can be found on the pattern pullout sheets.

Foundation patterns can have both numbers and letters. When more than one foundation is necessary to make a block, lowercase letters are included with each number. *Numbers indicate piecing order. Lowercase letters indicate the sections.* After piecing, sections are joined to make blocks.

Note

Even though you can often piece successfully in a different order, I've numbered the foundations so the seams will marry, if possible, when you join sections or blocks together.

Never cut on a line between matching lowercase letters. There are heavier lines around sections, but the letters are an additional aid to keeping things together, literally.

FOUNDATION PIECING PROCESS

Tip

Use a pencil to label the foundations for fabric placement.

1. Press or pin the first patch, *right side up*, into place on the plain (unprinted) side of the foundation. Make sure seam allowance extends at least ¼″ past all the boundary lines of patch 1.

 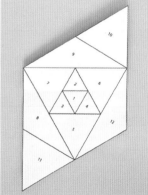

2. This is key! Place the foundation, printed side up, on a flat surface and fold on the line between patch 1 and patch 2. While the foundation is folded, there will be excess fabric extending past the fold. Trim it so it is only ¼″ beyond the fold. If you use freezer-paper foundations, you may have to peel the seam allowance away from the paper.

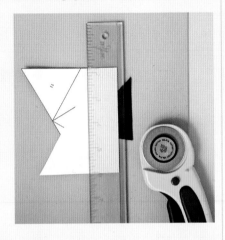

Tip

I had to be convinced to try this handy tool because I didn't want to give it space on my sewing table, but I'm glad I did. An Add-A-Quarter ruler, along with a small cutting mat and rotary cutter, are ideal for trimming. When working with non-freezer-paper foundations, laying the patch flat while you cut is easier and more accurate than using scissors.

3. Place patch 2 in position on patch 1, right sides together, lining up the edge of patch 2 with the trimmed edge of patch 1. Unfold the foundation.

4. Hold or pin the patches to the foundation, avoiding the stitching edge. Place the foundation printed side up under the presser foot.

5. *Shorten the stitch length* so it will perforate the paper adequately for removal later. Starting at least ¼″ away from the foundation, sew toward and onto the line between patches 1 and 2. Sew straight off the opposite end of the line and at least ¼″ onto the adjacent seam allowance.

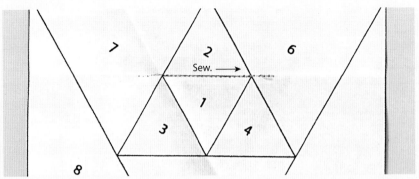

When a stitching line ends in the middle of the foundation, as in this demonstration, sew past the end of the line and onto the paper for at least ¼″. Take a couple of backstitches to anchor the thread. If you are chain piecing, just drag the foundation away from the needle until there's room for the next one in the chain.

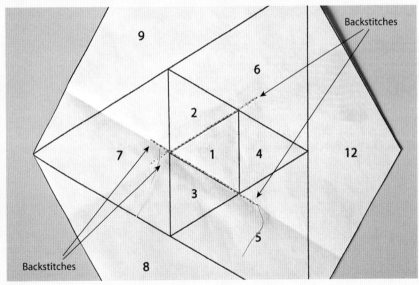

6. Set the seam after stitching. Please! Really, it makes a *huge difference*. See Tips for Pressing (page 27) for details.

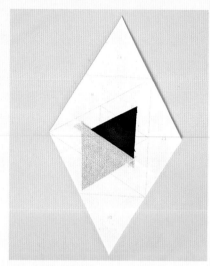

After adding patch 2, from the fabric side

7. Before adding patch 3, fold on the line between patch 2 and patch 3. Repeat the trimming process from Step 2. *This step is key.*

Backstitches

Tear stitches from the foundation when folding. Backstitches will keep the stitches from unraveling.

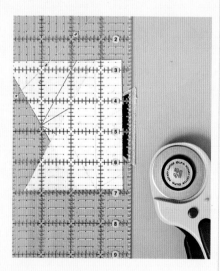

8. Turn the foundation over to the fabric side and put patch 3 in place, right sides together with patch 2, lining it up with the trimmed edge of patch 2. Unfold the foundation.

9. Hold or pin the patch in place. Turn over to the printed side of the foundation and stitch on the line. Press. Fold and trim.

Repeat with patch 4 and patch 5.

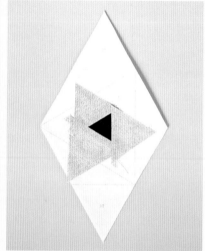

After adding patch 4, from the fabric side

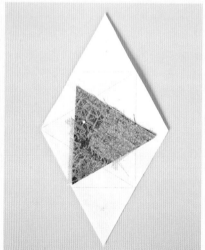

Pin patch 5.

10. And so on and "sew forth" until all the patches are in place.

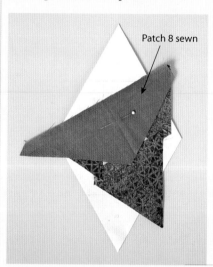

Patch 8 sewn

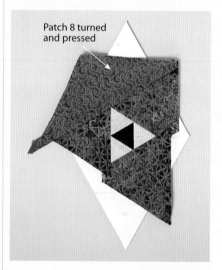

Patch 8 turned and pressed

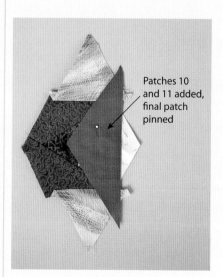

Patches 10 and 11 added, final patch pinned

11. Use the edge of the foundation as a guide and trim the blocks, adding a ¼" seam allowance on all sides.

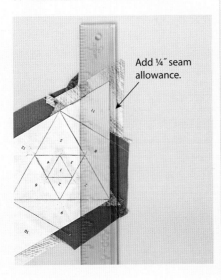

Add ¼" seam allowance.

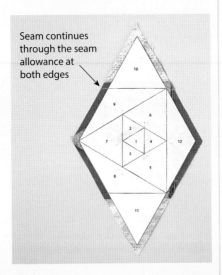

Seam continues through the seam allowance at both edges

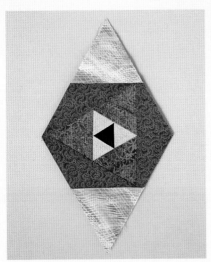

Completed block, from the fabric side

Tips

- Once you're confident of the steps, chain sewing will speed up the process tremendously!

- Grade the seam allowances when sewing a light fabric over a dark one. This will add a bit of extra coverage so the dark seam allowance will be covered completely by two layers of light. While not eliminating shadowing, it will make it less obvious.

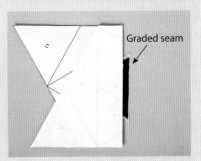

Graded seam

Grading fabric

- Machine baste near the edge of any loose or flapping patches on the foundations before joining. This ensures that the corners lie accurately in position.

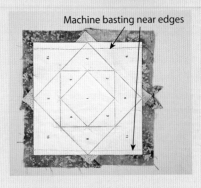

Machine basting near edges

12. Because foundations do not include a seam allowance, the papers can be left in place to stabilize the sections and units while the quilt is assembled. I leave the papers in place until they interfere with pressing; however, *all* papers must be removed before the quilt is layered.

PIN MATCHING

Careful pinning equals good matches. I haven't found a substitute. The thinner the pin, short of bending, the more pointy and accurate the matches will be. I use 0.5mm-diameter pins.

1. Place a pin (the "match pin") perpendicular to the sections, blocks, or units you're joining. The pin should be placed to go through the fewest layers of seam allowance possible, exactly at the match. Use the corners of the foundation as "dots" for matching. Foundations have a tick mark where a pieced seam meets a plain one.

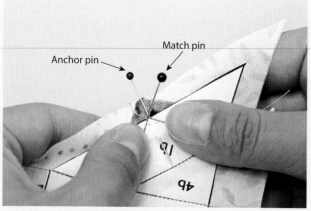

Bigger, untrimmed seam allowances are helpful.

2. While holding the match pin as upright as possible, insert another pin (the "anchor pin") to one side of the match pin. Insert the anchor pin flat, parallel to the surface of the fabric, so as not to disturb the match. Add a second anchor pin on the other side of the match pin.

3. Remove the match pin, and stitch with a normal stitch length. Do not sew over the pins if you value your sewing machine.

Tip

Accurate pinning can be easier if you wait to trim the seam allowances. The larger, un-trimmed edges give you something to hold on to and more fabric for anchoring pins. You can trim to ¼" after sewing.

WORKING WITH CURVED BAND TEMPLATES

Carefully trace curved band templates from the pullout masters onto freezer paper in the quantities required. Iron them to the wrong side of the fabric and add ¼" seam allowance as you cut. Mark a stitching line and any tick marks on the curves. If the band will be appliqued to the background, glue the seam allowance of the outside curve to the back of the freezer paper template. Before pinning, it is important to tear the band template, removing the inside curved edge. This makes it possible to sew the curve.

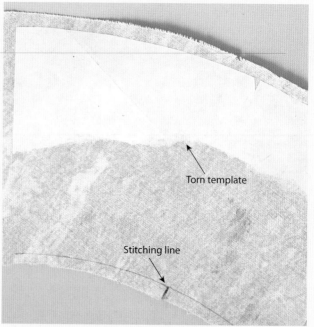

Notice that the template was used to mark the curved stitching line and ticks before the lower part of it was torn off.

PINNING AND SEWING CURVES

When I learned this technique from a student, I thought it was too easy to work. It does!

1. Place match pins at the tick marks to align the curves you are joining. Put in as many match pins at a time as you can manage.

2. One of the layers will be lying fairly flat, while the other will begin to form ruffles. Work with the misbehaving fabric on top, where you can see it.

3. Insert anchor pins within the arc, pointing toward the stitching line. Push each pin in until the point comes up to, but doesn't cross, the stitching line. Test alignment by stabbing a pin into the stitching line to check that it emerges on the stitching line on the facing side. If it doesn't, do more pinning.

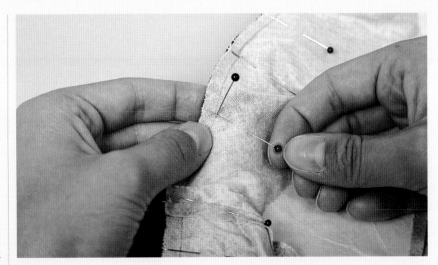

Tip
If you need more reference points for matches, fold the fabric layers, lining up the ticks already there, and pinch in a pleat on the arc. Repeat between pleats if needed.

4. Sew with the misbehaving fabric on top, as you did while pinning. Sew the curved seam, steering into the curve as you go. Use a slightly shortened stitch length to make turning easier. *Do not clip the seam allowances*; you'll get a nicer curve if you don't.

5. Remove the pins, check the seam, and adjust if necessary. Press seam allowances toward the outside of the arc.

"DOUGHNUT HOLE" APPLIQUÉ

The medallions in the quilt designs use my unusual method to appliqué the centers in place. Once the arcs of the medallion are joined, there is an empty space in the center—a "doughnut hole." Turn the medallion wrong side up and iron it flat. Cover the hole with a piece of freezer paper. Press in place. Turn the medallion right side up and use a ruler to find and mark the center. Use the seams to align the ruler.

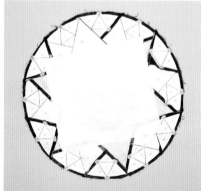

The center circles are made with freezer-paper templates. Fold the outer seam allowance to the back of the template, and use a gluestick to adhere the seam allowance to the back of the template. Make sure the edge doesn't have tucks or pleats. Use a pin to line up the circle's center with the center mark on the doughnut hole.

Put dots of basting glue on the circle's seam allowance and press it onto the medallion while the centers are aligned.

Use invisible thread to appliqué the circle to the medallion. I use the methods described by Harriet Hargrave in *Mastering Machine Appliqué*.

"Paint" the glued seam allowance with water to soften and release the glue. Remove the freezer-paper template.

MATCHING BANDS TO QUILT UNITS

Before adding bands to the patchwork units, make marks on the seam allowances where the block's seams should land. Remember to allow for the seam allowance at the start of marking.

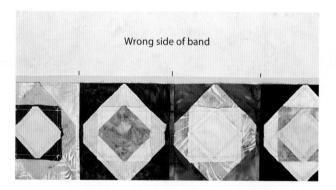

Wrong side of band

For example, if you are joining the band to a section of 6″ blocks, start with a small mark on the seam allowance, ¼″ from the end of the band (the "dot"). Then, 6″ from the dot, make a mark on the band's seam allowance. Continue down the band, spacing marks 6″ apart until you've defined the positions of the seams in the adjoining unit. If the band crosses another band or unit, adjust the marking distances accordingly. See *Portico Pavement*, Quilt Assembly, Step 1, for an example (page 58).

TIPS FOR PRESSING

I can't emphasize enough how important it is to press each seam, especially during the foundation piecing process. Why go to the bother of sewing carefully on a precise line if you press in a pleat, effectively moving that line?

Tip

Chain piece the patches, and then get up from the sewing table and go to the ironing board to press them all at the same time. It's good for your body and allows you to press efficiently.

Set the seams—it's *magic*! Press the seam closed, the way it came out from under the machine. Then press the patch over and open, to its place, with the *side* of the iron. If you're foundation piecing, check to see that there's no pleat, because after you add the next patch, you won't want to try to fix it. *Verify that you have an adequate seam allowance at this juncture too.*

I like to use the shot-of-steam button on my iron, but I don't pull or force the fabric—I just get a nice sharp crease and flatten the fabric.

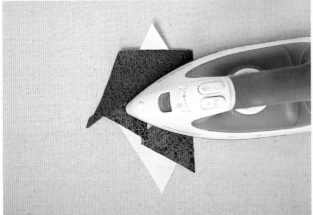

Press each seam flat before pressing it open.

Tip

Married seams make it easier to join sections and blocks accurately. To marry seams, you may want to interrupt the piecing process to trim a section and remove the paper so that you can change the direction a seam is pressed. If you do, set the seam again.

It's not possible to marry *all* seams. Where they can't be married, pin matching (page 24) is even more important. If many seam allowances are piling up at a match point, press the seams open after stitching, distributing the bulk more evenly on the surface.

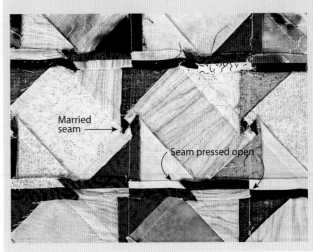

Married seam →

Seam pressed open

CIAO BELLA!

Ciao Bella! / Hello Beautiful!, 60″ × 60″, by Norah McMeeking, quilted by Kim Peterson of Kimberwood Quilting

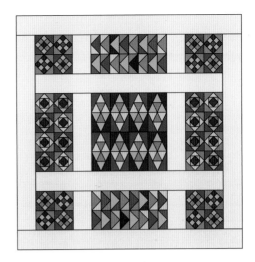

This quilt is built on a simple 5″ grid. The center is 20″ × 20″, the rectangles that surround it are each 10″ × 20″, and the plain corner blocks are 10″ × 10″.

Preselected medleys are great for beginners or those of us who love bundles, but make sure the medley you choose has a full range of dark to light fabric. *Ciao Bella!* is made with a fourteen-piece bundle of Hoffman fat quarters (the Jasmine collection). I added more yardage for the 5″ bands and for the plain corner squares. For wider choice and to allow for mistakes or changes, I suggest you buy a duplicate fat-quarter bundle and use leftovers in other projects.

You may also assemble a fabric palette from your stash, gathering various fabrics to equal at least three yards. Read Choosing Fabric (page 12) for advice on assembling a palette.

Before you begin, think about how you might vary this design:

- Replace the rectangle units with plain fabric, adding appliqué designs instead.

- Use patchwork in all the units.

- Place a compass in the center or plan blocks to make a unified design, as in my quilt.

- Change the blocks' colors, orientation, or both, or cut down work by alternating plain squares cut to size.

- Choose a gorgeous print for the corner squares or rectangles.

- Unify the design by making all the rectangle units from the same block.

- Choose different blocks.

In my sample quilt the center is made of 25 squares 4″ × 4″, but you could change it to 16 squares 5″ × 5″ or 4 squares 10″ × 10″. Look through the pattern pullouts at the back of the book and choose the blocks *you* like the most. While I encourage you to do your own thing, the following instructions describe how I made *Ciao Bella!*

Fabric and Cutting Requirements

Backing and binding: 4¼ yards

Batting: 68″ × 68″

FLYING GEESE

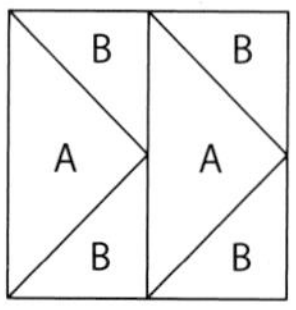

Make 8 blocks
5″ × 5″ finished.

PATCH		FABRIC	CUTTING SIZE	QUANTITY	TOTAL PATCHES
A	⊠	¼ yard mixed light, medium, and dark batiks	7″ × 7″	4	16
B	◹	¼ yard mixed light, medium, and dark batiks	4½″ × 4½″	16	32

POISED SQUARE-IN-A-SQUARE

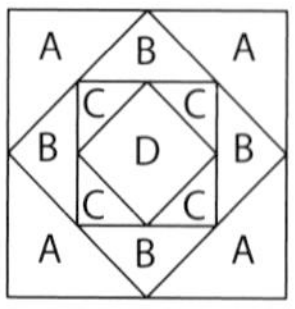

Make 8 blocks
5″ × 5″ finished.

PATCH		FABRIC	CUTTING SIZE	QUANTITY	TOTAL PATCHES
A	◹	¼ yard mixed dark and medium batiks	4″ × 4″	16	32
B	⊠	⅜ yard mixed light batiks	5″ × 5″	8	32
C	◹	¼ yard mixed medium batiks	3″ × 3″	16	32
D	☐	1 strip 2¾″ × WOF dark batik	2¾″ × 2¾″	8	8

POISED NINE-PATCH

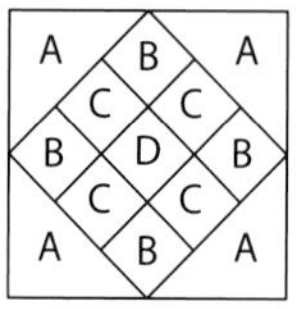

Make 8 blocks
5″ × 5″ finished.

PATCH		FABRIC	CUTTING SIZE	QUANTITY	TOTAL PATCHES
A	◹	¼ yard mixed dark and medium batiks	4″ × 4″	16	32
B	☐	1 strip 2″ × WOF dark batik, 1 strip 2″ × WOF light batik	2″ × 2″	16 from each strip	32
C	☐	1 strip 2″ × WOF medium batik, 1 strip 2″ × WOF light batik	2″ × 2″	16 from each strip	32
D	☐	1 strip 2″ × WOF dark batik	2″ × 2″	8	8

PALIO PENNANT

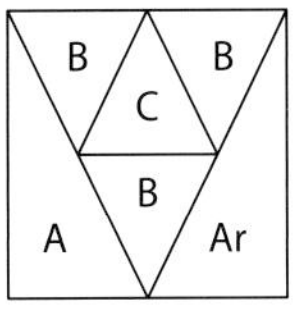

Make 8 blocks
5" × 5" finished.

PATCH		FABRIC	CUTTING SIZE	QUANTITY	TOTAL PATCHES
A and Ar	CT	2 dark batiks totaling ¼ yard	6¾" × 18"	2	16
B	CT	2 light batiks totaling ¼ yard	4" × 26"	2	24
C	CT	2 medium batiks totaling ⅛ yard	4" × 12"	2	8

TURNING TRIANGLES

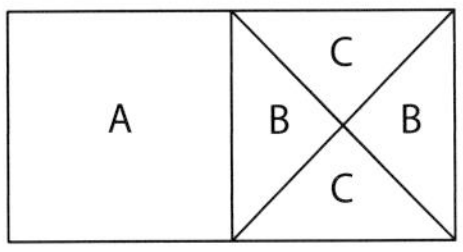

Make 12 pieced blocks and 13 alternate plain blocks, each 4" × 4" finished.

PATCH		FABRIC	CUTTING SIZE	QUANTITY	TOTAL PATCHES
A	▢	1 strip 5" × WOF medium batik, 1 strip 5" × 20" bright batik, 1 square 5" × 5" dark batik	5" × 5"	8 from medium, 4 from bright, 1 from dark	13
B	◻	1 strip 6½" × WOF light batik	6½" × 6½"	6	24
C	◻	1 strip 6½" × 26" dark batik, 1 strip 6½" × 13" different dark batik	6½" × 6½"	4 from 1 batik, 2 from the other batik	24

BANDS AND CORNER SQUARES

BAND*	FABRIC	CUTTING SIZE	QUANTITY
A	2 yards lightest batik	5½" × 10½"	4
B		5½" × 20½"	2
C		5½" × 50½"	4
D		5½" × 60½"	2
Corner squares	⅝ yard burgundy	10½" × 10½"	4

Cut all bands on length of grain.

Paper Foundations

Read General Instructions (pages 17–27) before starting.

*N*ote

CAUTION

Remember that stitching lines are on what will be the *wrong side* of the completed block. Keep that reversal in mind when color placement varies or blocks have a direction (like Flying Geese).

Foundation Piecing

FLYING GEESE

1. Trace or copy 8 foundations from pattern pullout page P1.

2. Tape or glue 4 foundations in a row, and piece in numbered order. Trim the row, leaving a ¼" seam allowance.

3. Make 2 rows and join them.

POISED SQUARE-IN-A-SQUARE

1. Trace or copy 8 foundations from pattern pullout page P1.

2. Piece in numbered order.

3. Make 2 rows of 4 blocks each and then join the rows.

POISED NINE-PATCH

1. Trace or copy 8 foundations from pattern pullout page P1.

2. Cut the paper foundation into sections for piecing, as shown. Even though they are only single shapes, use foundations for the 2 quarter-square triangles. The foundations have tick marks for matching, and the edge of the foundation will be used to trim to size.

3. Piece sections a, b, and c in numbered order, and sew them together. The seams should marry.

4. Add D triangles to each side. Match tick marks printed on foundations to the corresponding seams. Match corners too.

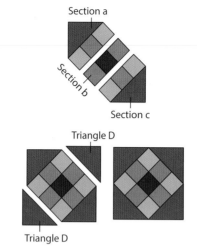

Section a

Section b

Section c

Triangle D

Triangle D

5. Make 2 rows of 4 blocks each and join them.

PALIO PENNANT

1. Trace or copy 8 foundations from pattern pullout page P1.

2. Piece in numbered order.

3. Make 2 rows of 4 blocks each and then join the rows.

TURNING TRIANGLES

1. Trace or copy 13 foundations from pattern pullout page P1, and cut 3 of them apart on the line between 2b and 3b. Discard one of the foundations for the pieced block.

2. Cut the paper foundation into sections for piecing, as shown.

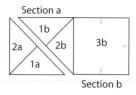

Section a

2a | 1b | 3b
| 2b |
1a

Section b

3. Piece sections a and b in numbered order, using the quilt photo (below, and on page 28) and the following illustrations to guide color placement, and sew them together. The seams should marry.

4. Join the units to make rows. Make 2 of Row 1, 2 of Row 2, and 1 of Row 3.

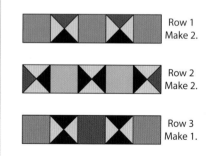

Row 1
Make 2.

Row 2
Make 2.

Row 3
Make 1.

5. Sew the rows together to complete the center unit.

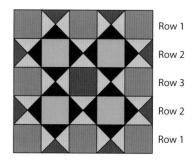

Row 1

Row 2

Row 3

Row 2

Row 1

Bands and Final Assembly

1. Sew a band A to each side of the Palio Pennant unit and to each side of the Flying Geese unit. Add a corner square to the remaining sides of band A.

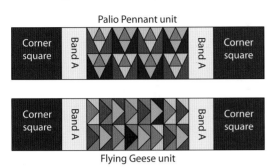

2. Sew a band B to each side of the center. Then add the Poised Square-in-a-Square unit to one side and the Poised Nine-Patch unit to the other side.

3. Sew a band C to the top of the center and another to the bottom.

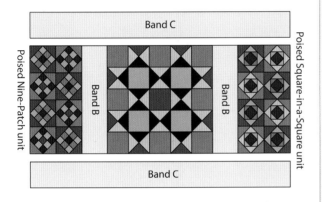

4. Add the Palio Pennant unit to the top of the center, and add the Flying Geese unit to the bottom.

5. Sew a band C to each side of the center. Finally, sew a band D to the top and bottom to complete the quilt top.

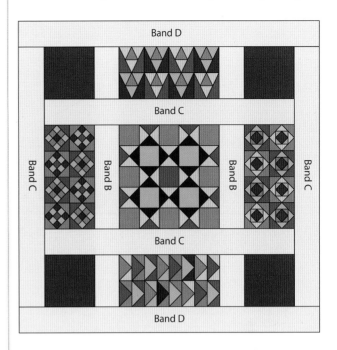

Optional Embroidery

If you want to add the impression of weaving to the bands of the quilt, embroider a dark line ¼″ from the edges of the bands. *It is necessary to secure some type of stabilizer to the back of the bands before you begin.* Freezer paper works for me, as does the built-in double backstitch function (forward, back, forward; stitch #02 on my Pfaff.) Use contrasting-color thread of your choice. Study the photo of *Ciao Bella!* (page 28) for placement.

VITERBO

Viterbo, 64" × 64", by Norah McMeeking and the Bella Brigade, quilted by Kim Peterson of Kimberwood Quilting

Viterbo, just north of Rome, was built by the Etruscans and was once the papal seat. Inside two walls, its town center is filled with winding, narrow streets, old fountains, ancient bridges, and tiny cars.

Before you begin, think about how you might vary this design:

- Use 3" or 6" blocks.

- Make every square unit from a different block.

- Place a compass in the center of a 16" square and surround it with 4" blocks in the center unit.

- Replace the triangles with plain fabric or a fabulous print.

- Appliqué a design to plain triangles in place of the patchwork.

This design is based on units of 12″ × 12″ squares and half-squares, all made of 4″ blocks, but you could substitute 3″ × 3″ or 6″ × 6″ blocks. The center unit is 24″ × 24″ and might be made with 2″ × 2″, 4″ × 4″, 6″ × 6″, or 8″ × 8″ blocks. The surrounding triangles made up of Venetian Pavers measure 16″ on the square sides. While I encourage you to change this design to suit your tastes, the following directions describe how I made *Viterbo*.

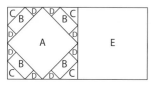

Fabric and Cutting Requirements

Backing and binding: 4¾ yards

Batting: 72″ × 72″

FORUM STEPS

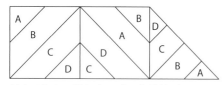

Make 20 pieced blocks and 16 plain blocks, each 4″ × 4″ finished.

	PATCH	FABRIC	CUTTING SIZE	QUANTITY	TOTAL PATCHES
A	☐	¼ yard mixed medium-lights	4″ × 4″	20	20
B	☐	⅓ yard mixed lights	1¾″ × 2½″	80	80
C	◨	¼ yard mixed darks and mediums	2½″ × 2½″	40	80
D	⊠	⅜ yard mixed darks and mediums	3¼″ × 3¼″	40	160
E	☐	¼ yard mixed mediums	4½″ × 4½″	16	16

VENETIAN PAVERS / TRIANGLE

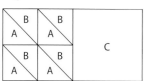

Make 24 pieced blocks and 16 half-blocks, each 4″ × 4″ finished.

For this block, you need four contrasting fabrics from dark to light in value. I used beige, brown, green, and white Stonehenge fabrics from Northcott. Piece this block using paper foundations and strips rather than preshaped patches. If you plan to vary this design, matching units are easiest to make.

COLOR	YARDAGE	CUT STRIPS	QUANTITY
Beige	½ yard	2½″ × 40″	6
Brown	½ yard	2½″ × 40″	6
Green	½ yard	2½″ × 40″	6
White	½ yard	2½″ × 40″	6

COSMATI REFLECTIONS / CENTER SQUARE

Make 18 pieced blocks and 18 plain blocks, each 4″ × 4″ finished.

	PATCH	FABRIC	CUTTING SIZE	QUANTITY	TOTAL PATCHES
A	◨	½ yard mixed darks and lights	3½″ × 3½″	36	72
B	◨	½ yard mixed lights and darks	3½″ × 3½″	36	72
C	☐	Light and medium batiks totaling ½ yard	5″ × 5″	18	18

BANDS

BAND*	FABRIC	CUTTING SIZE	QUANTITY
A	1¾ yards light	2½″ × 12½″	4
B and Br		2½″ × 12⅞″	2 each
C		2½″ × 16½″	4
D		2½″ × 18⅞″	4
E		2½″ × 20⅞″	4
F		2½″ × 24½″	2
G		2½″ × 56½″	2

* Cut all bands on length of grain.

Use the 45° angle on a quilter's ruler to trim a triangle off the end of bands B, Br, D, and E. Angle the ruler to cut bands, slanting as shown below.

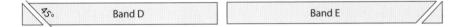

BACKGROUND AND BORDERS

	FABRIC	CUTTING SIZE	QUANTITY	TOTAL PIECES
Background triangles 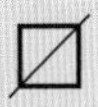	2 yards dark	12⅞″ × 12⅞″	4	8
Borders		4½″ × 56½″	2	2
		4½″ × 64½″	2	2

Paper Foundations

Read General Instructions (pages 17–27) before starting.

Note

Remember that stitching lines are on what will be the *wrong side* of the completed block. Keep that reversal in mind when color placement varies or blocks have a direction (such as Cosmati Reflections).

Foundation Piecing
FORUM STEPS

1. Trace or copy 20 foundations from pattern pullout page P1.

2. Cut the paper foundation into 4 sections for piecing. Notice that one corner stays attached to the center.

3. Piece each section in numbered order.

4. Add the small triangle sections to the larger foundation, pin matching the tick mark to the point and the edges of the foundations together.

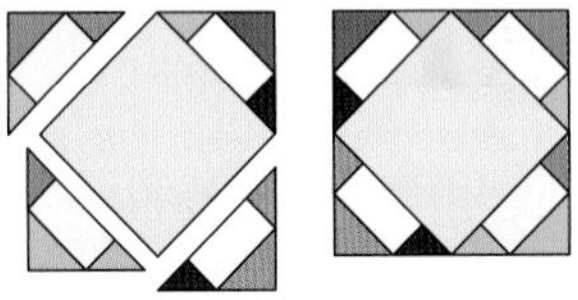

5. Make 8 rows by alternating 2 Forum Steps blocks with a plain 4½″ × 4½″ square (Row 1), and 4 rows by alternating 2 plain squares with a Forum Steps block (Row 2).

6. Make 4 square sections by sewing alternating rows together.

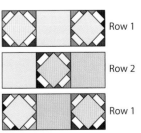

Row 1

Row 2

Row 1

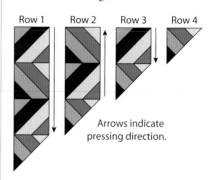

VENETIAN PAVERS / TRIANGLES

This simple block takes on life when you turn it this way and that to make a pattern.

1. Trace or copy 32 foundations from pattern pullout page P1.

2. Carefully draw a line across 8 of the foundations to divide them in half across the strips diagonally. Cut on the line to make 16 triangle foundations.

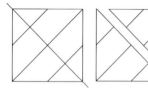

3. Arrange the foundations into 4 triangular sections. Carefully label each foundation in pencil for fabric placement. Because they are in reverse, this can get confusing, so take your time!

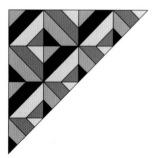

Venetian Pavers block, front view

Make 8.

Make 16.

Make 16.

4. Follow the marked labels carefully and piece in numbered order, using strips. Be sure you allow for the length required when sewing the patch 2 fabric in place. It's easy to forget! Remember that the front of the foundation will be a mirror image of the labeled foundations.

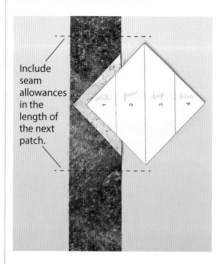

Include seam allowances in the length of the next patch.

Note

When positioning the strip to cover patch 2, be sure to allow enough width to cover the corners.

Tip

Before joining the sections together, play with them a bit, just to see what happens. In fact, do that with *all* the blocks!

5. Assemble rows, and then join them to make the triangle units.

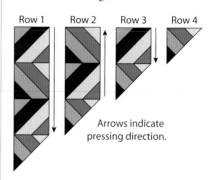

Arrows indicate pressing direction.

COSMATI REFLECTIONS / CENTER

1. Trace or copy 18 foundations from pattern pullout page P1.

2. Cut the paper foundation into 2 sections, and foundation piece each section in numbered order to allow seams to marry when sections are joined. Reverse the placement of the light and dark triangles in half the blocks, so triangles will face the same direction in each row. See the illustrations (below and on next page) to guide light/dark color placement.

Section a

Section b

3. Join the blocks into rows making sure the dark triangles point the same direction. Sew the rows together.

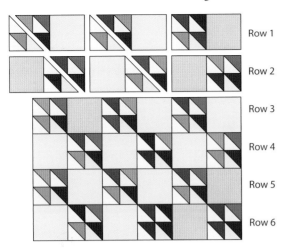

Row 1
Row 2
Row 3
Row 4
Row 5
Row 6

Quilt Assembly

1. Sew a band A to the outside edge of each square unit. Sew band B/Br to the opposite side. Press the seams toward the band. Sew band C to the top edge.

Trimmed band B   Trimmed band Br

2. Sew a band D to the left side of 2 Venetian Paver / Triangle units and a band E to the right (not shown separately).

3. Sew a background triangle to each band B/Br so that the units are mirror images of each other. Add these units to the Venetian Paver / Triangle units to complete the top and bottom sections of the quilt.

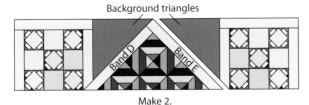

Background triangles

Make 2.

4. Sew background triangles to bands D and E of the remaining triangle units, matching the dot of the background triangle's point to the corner dot of the bands. The bands will extend past the unit as shown.

5. Align a quilter's ruler with the edge of the background triangle and trim triangles off the extensions on bands D and E to form a rectangle.

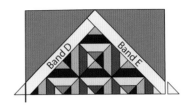

6. Sew band F to opposite sides of the Cosmati Reflections / Center unit. Add the remaining units to each side to complete the middle row of the quilt.

7. Sew band G to the top and bottom edges of the middle row. Sew the top and bottom rows to band G.

8. Sew the short border strips to opposite sides of the quilt top. Sew the longer border strips to the top and bottom to complete the quilt top.

LATERANO INTERLACE

Laterano Interlace, 64" × 64", by Norah McMeeking, quilted by Paula Rostkowski of A Quilter's Work

This quilt is based on a section of floor in San Giovanni Laterano in Rome. The cathedral is the seat of the bishop of Rome, who is also the pope. Built atop the ancient quarters of the Roman cavalry bodyguard, the property was given to the pope by the emperor Constantine in the fourth century. The cathedral is one of the most spectacular buildings in the city.

Before you begin, consider how you might vary this design:

- Fill the rectangles and 10″ squares with appliquéd motifs.
- Replace the rectangles and squares with patchwork.
- Use a simple 2″ square in place of the Poised Square block.

While I encourage you to change this design to suit your tastes, the following directions describe how I made *Laterano Interlace*.

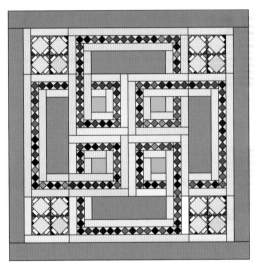

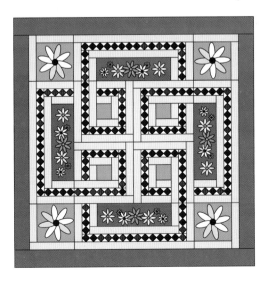

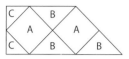

Fabric and Cutting Requirements

Backing and binding: 4¾ yards

Batting: 72″ × 72″

POISED SQUARE BORDERS

Make 168 border units 2″ × 2″.

PATCH		FABRIC	CUTTING SIZE	QUANTITY	TOTAL PATCHES
A	□	1 yard mixed bright and medium batiks	2¾″ × 2¾″	168	168
B	⊠	⅞ yard mixed dark brown batiks	4″ × 4″	70	280
C	◻	⅜ yard mixed dark brown batiks	2½″ × 2½″	56	112

BACKGROUND SQUARES AND RECTANGLES, AND BORDERS

PATCH	FABRIC	CUTTING SIZE	QUANTITY	TOTAL PATCHES
Background 1 □	⅝ yards brown #1	4½″ × 4½″	4	4
		10½″ × 10½″	4	4
Background 2 ▭	2 yards brown #2	6½″ × 20½″	4	4
		4½″ × 56½″	2	2
		4½″ × 64½″	2	2

BANDS

BAND*	FABRIC	CUTTING SIZE	QUANTITY
A	1¾ yards mixed light batiks	2½″ × 4½″	4
B		2½″ × 6½″	16
C		2½″ × 8½″	4
D		2½″ × 12½″	8
E		2½″ × 14½″	8
F		2½″ × 16½″	4
G		2½″ × 24½″	4
H		2½″ × 10½″	12
I		2½″ × 32½″	4

* Cut all bands on length of grain.

Paper Foundations

Read General Instructions (pages 17–27) before starting.

*N*ote

CAUTION

Remember that stitching lines are on what will be the *wrong side* of the completed block.

Foundation Piecing

1. The foundations on pullout page P1 have blocks grouped in triples, quadruples, and end sections. Trace or copy 28 of each end unit, 8 triples, and 28 quadruples. From each of 8 quadruples, cut a single and a triple. From each of 4 quadruples, cut doubles. You should have 8 singles, 8 doubles, 8 triples, and 16 quadruples—enough to make all the following units.

2. Piece the foundations in numbered order, and sew the sections together to form the following units.

Unit 1—Make 4.

Unit 2—Make 8.

Unit 3—Make 4.

Unit 4—Make 8.

Unit 5—Make 4.

Unit Assembly

This quilt is made up of two main units, the Log Cabin–style units and the side units. You will need four of each. Begin the Log Cabin–style units (so named because they assemble in much the same way as a Log Cabin block) from the center out.

CENTER BLOCKS

1. Sew band A to the top edge of the smaller background square.

2. Add band B to the side, as shown, before adding another band B to the bottom.

3. Sew unit 1 to the top of the section and unit 2 to the side.

4. Continue to add foundation units and bands until you've completed a center block.

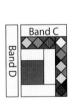
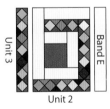
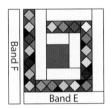

5. Repeat Steps 1–4 to make a total of 4 center blocks. All the blocks should look alike.

6. Rotate the completed blocks as shown and join to complete the center of the quilt.

RECTANGLE UNITS

1. Sew a band B to each end of a 6½″ × 20½″ background rectangle, and add band G to the top.

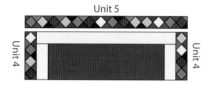

2. Sew a unit 4 to each side and unit 5 to band G.

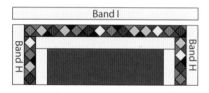

3. Add band H to each end and band I to the top to complete the rectangle unit. Make 4.

CORNER UNITS

Sew band H to the side of the large background square. Add band D to the top. Make 3 more.

Quilt Assembly

1. Add a rectangle unit to opposite sides of the center unit.

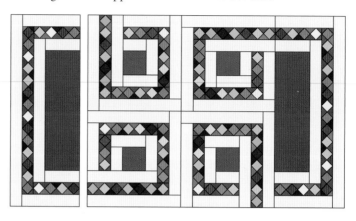

2. Add a corner unit to opposite sides of the remaining rectangle units.

3. Join the units together and add borders to complete the top.

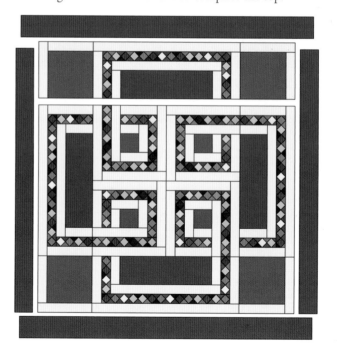

SALERNO SAMPLER

Salerno Sampler, 75" × 75", by Norah McMeeking, quilted by Dee Angus of Tomorrow's Treasures

This quilt provides plenty of opportunities to vary the design because its 15″ units accommodate both 3″ and 5″ blocks. I suggest you begin by making two or three square units. Fold them diagonally in halves and quarters to decide if you want to work with triangle units as well as square ones.

Before you begin, think about how you might vary this design:

- Make four compasses for the squares, leaving the center square plain.
- Place patchwork in the triangle spaces as well as the squares.
- Use a printed panel in the squares.
- Replace the pieced border with a colorful print and use that print to build the fabric palette.

This design is composed of poised 15″ squares, each of which might be made with 25 squares, each 3″ × 3″, or with 9 squares, each 5″ × 5″. Look through the pattern pullouts at the back of the book and choose the blocks *you* like the most. Though I encourage you to do your own thing with this design, the following describes how I made *Salerno Sampler*.

Fabric and Cutting Requirements

Backing and binding: 7¾ yards

Batting: 83″ × 83″

Tip

Before starting the piecing, cut at least three or four 2″ strips of each fabric in your palette and set them aside to use in the border blocks.

DOUBLE COSMATI TRIANGLE

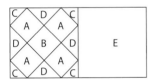

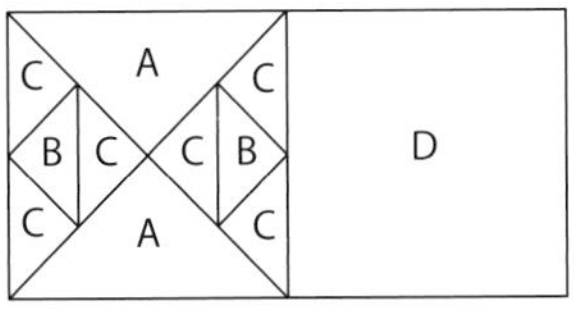

Make 12 pieced blocks and 13 plain blocks, each 3″ × 3″ finished.

PATCH		FABRIC	CUTTING SIZE	QUANTITY	TOTAL PATCHES
A	⊠	¼ yard mixed light fabrics	5″ × 5″	6	24
B	⊠	⅛ yard yellow	3½″ × 3½″	6	24
C	⊠	¼ yard mixed dark fabrics	3½″ × 3½″	18	72
D	☐	¼ yard mixed medium fabrics	3½″ × 3½″	13	13

TRIP TO ROME

Make 13 pieced blocks and 12 plain blocks, each 3″ × 3″ finished.

PATCH		FABRIC	CUTTING SIZE	QUANTITY	TOTAL PATCHES
A	☐	¼ yard mixed light fabrics	1¾″ × 1¾″	52	52
B	☐	⅛ yard bright and dark scraps	2″ × 2″	13	13
C	◹	¼ yard mixed dark fabrics	2″ × 2″	26	52
D	⊠		3½″ × 3½″	13	52
E	☐	¼ yard mixed golds	3½″ × 3½″	12	12

HEXAGON STAR

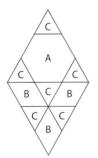

Make 5 rows using 15 of these blocks and additional "filler" sections.

PATCH		FABRIC	CUTTING SIZE	QUANTITY*	TOTAL PATCHES
A	⬡	⅜ yard mixed bright and medium fabrics	3″ strips cut as described in Cutting Other Shapes (page 17)	3 strips	25 (20 whole, 5 partial)
B	▱60°	⅜ yard mixed dark fabrics	2″ strips cut as described in Cutting Other Shapes (page 17)	5 strips	71 (60 whole, 11 partial)
C	◿	⅜ yard mixed light fabrics	2¼″ strips cut as described in Cutting Other Shapes (page 17)	5 strips	135 (126 whole, 9 partial)

* Quantity depends on number of colors/fabrics used.

SQUARE-IN-A-DIAMOND

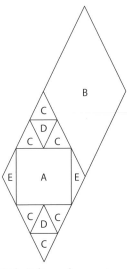

Make 7 diagonal rows using the units shown on page 50.

PATCH		FABRIC	CUTTING SIZE	QUANTITY*	TOTAL PATCHES
A	☐	⅛ yard mixed medium and bright scraps	2¾" × 2¾"	10	10
Half-A	▭		2¾" × 1¾"	5	5
B	CT	¼ yard mixed scraps	3½" × 40" strip	1 strip	8 full
Vertical half-B	T		3½" × 20" strip	1 strip	4 vertical halves
Horizontal half-B	T		3½" × 12" strip	1 strip	4 horizontal halves
Quarter-B	T		3½" × 5" strip	1 strip	2
C	CT	½ yard mixed light fabrics	2¼" × 40" strips	3 strips	75
D	CT	Mixed dark scraps	2¼" × 40" strip	1 strip	25
E	CT				
Vertical half-E	CT		1½" × 40" strips	2 strips	30 (20E, 10F)

* Quantity depends on number of colors/fabrics used.

EVENING STAR / *STELLA DI SERA* COMPASS

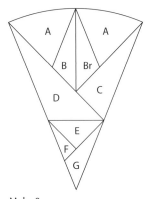

Make 8.

PATCH		FABRIC	CUTTING SIZE	QUANTITY	TOTAL PATCHES
A	CT	¼ yard light	4" × 24" strip	2 strips	16
E	◪		3¼" × 3¼"	2	8
B	CT	⅛ yard tan	3½" × 20" strip	1 strip	8
Br	CT	⅛ yard red	3½" × 20" strip	1 strip	8
F	CT		2" × 14" strip	1 strip	8
C	CT	⅛ yard gold	4" × 20" strip	1 strip	8
G	CT		3½" × 10" strip	1 strip	4
		⅛ yard dark brown	3½" × 10" strip	1 strip	4
D	CT		4" × 30" strip	1 strip	8

VENETIAN PAVERS BORDER

 Tip

Cut 2" strips from every fabric you are using in the quilt. You'll need about 78 strips, or 4⅓ yards total, for the border blocks.

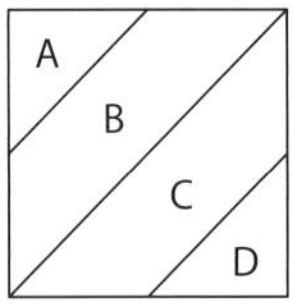

Make 176 blocks using 2" strips. These blocks finish slightly less than 2⅞" × 2⅞".

SETTING TRIANGLES AND COMPASS BACKGROUND

PATCH		FABRIC	CUTTING SIZE	QUANTITY	TOTAL PATCHES
Triangle A	◻	1 yard medium taupe	11½″ × 11½″	2	4
Triangle B	◻		22½″ × 22½″	1	4
Compass background	T			4	4

BANDS

BAND*	FABRIC	CUTTING SIZE	QUANTITY
A	2⅞ yards beige	3½″ × 15½″	6
B		3½″ × 22¼″	4
C		3½″ × 51½″	2
D		3½″ × 51½″	2
E		3½″ × 57½″	2
F		3½″ × 69½″	2
G		3½″ × 75½″	2

Cut all bands on length of grain.

Paper Foundations

Read General Instructions (pages 17–27) before starting.

CAUTION

Remember that stitching lines are on what will be the *wrong side* of the completed block. Keep that reversal in mind when color placement varies or blocks have a direction (like the Double Cosmati Triangle blocks).

Foundation Piecing

DOUBLE COSMATI TRIANGLES

1. Trace or copy 12 foundations from pattern pullout page P1.

2. Piece in numbered order.

This foundation has 2 sections. Join them on the diagonal. The seams will marry.

Make 12.

3. Join in rows with alternating plain squares, paying attention to make sure the orientation of the pieced block is correct.

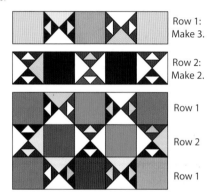

Row 1: Make 3.
Row 2: Make 2.
Row 1
Row 2
Row 1

TRIP TO ROME

1. Trace or copy 13 foundations from pattern pullout page P1.

2. Piece in numbered order.

This block has 3 sections. The seams will marry if pieced as numbered.

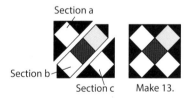

Section a
Section b
Section c   Make 13.

3. Join in rows with alternating plain squares.

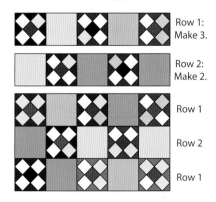

Row 1: Make 3.
Row 2: Make 2.
Row 1
Row 2
Row 1

HEXAGON STAR

This "block" is a diamond shape made of three sections. The diagrams show the sections from the front, but foundation lines are on the back and so are reversed. Remember that and you won't get confused.

1. Trace or copy 15 foundations from pattern pullout page P2. These are for the full "blocks"; the other foundations provided are for the filler sections in Step 3.

2. Piece in numbered order.

As each section is completed, use the edge of the foundation as a guide to trim it, leaving a ¼" seam allowance on all sides. Carefully remove the papers.

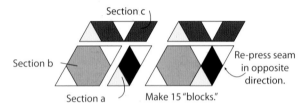

After removing the foundation papers, re-pressing the seam as shown makes joining the sections easier.

3. Trace and copy additional foundation sections in the quantities shown below, and make filler sections to complete the rows.

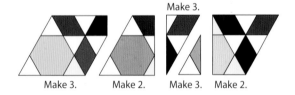

4. To complete the unit, assemble the "blocks" into rows as follows:

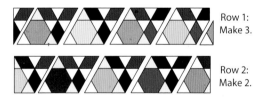

5. Join the rows to complete the unit.

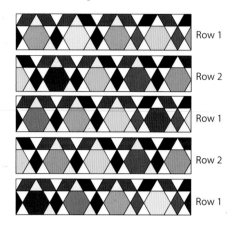

SQUARE-IN-A-DIAMOND

The alternating plain diamond is part of section a in this two-section foundation.

1. Trace or copy foundations from pattern pullout page P2 using the quantities shown below. There are 8 full "blocks"; the other foundations provided are for the filler sections.

2. Piece in numbered order to make units and partial units as shown.

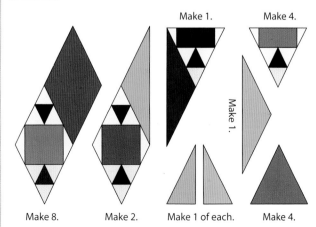

3. Join them in diagonal rows.

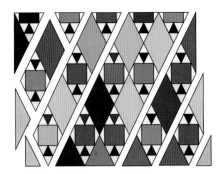

EVENING STAR / *STELLA DI SERA* COMPASS

You may be surprised at how easily this striking compass goes together.

1. Trace or copy 4 foundations from pattern pullout page P1.

2. Piece in numbered order.

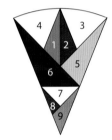

Make 8. Remember that patch 9 can be one of two different fabrics.

3. Join the foundations in pairs. Press the joining seam in the same direction on all 4 pairs so that the seams will eventually marry.

4. Sew a curved seam to add the background corner to each pair. See Pinning and Sewing Curves (page 25) for important tips on curved seams.

5. Join the quarters into halves. *If the center points don't match at this stage, this is the time to fix the problem.* Press the seams so they keep going in the same direction.

6. Join the halves together to complete the unit.

BORDER

1. Trace or copy 176 foundations from pattern pullout page P1.

2. Piece in numbered order, placing the fabrics randomly.

3. Join 20 blocks, rotating them so that the seams marry and the pattern makes a zigzag design. Make 2 of row 1 and 2 of row 2, paying attention to the orientation of the diagonals. Arrange the rows in pairs, pressing the seams that join them in opposing directions. Sew the pairs together to make the side border units.

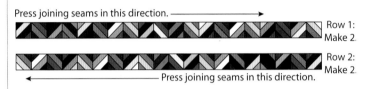

Press joining seams in this direction. ⟶

Row 1: Make 2.

Row 2: Make 2.

⟵ Press joining seams in this direction.

4. For the top and bottom borders, repeat Step 3 using 24 blocks per row, again paying attention to the orientation of the diagonals.

Quilt Assembly

1. Sew a band A to opposite sides of the Double Cosmati Triangle unit. Sew a band A to opposite sides of the Trip to Rome unit.

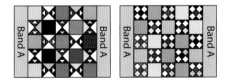

2. Sew a band A to opposite sides of the Evening Star Compass unit. Then sew the Square-in-a-Diamond unit to a band A and the Hexagon Star unit to the other, as diagrammed.

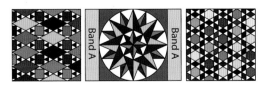

3. Use the 45° line on a quilter's ruler to carefully trim off the corners of 4 band B's.

4. Sew a triangle B to opposite sides of both the Double Cosmati Triangle unit and the Trip to Rome unit, positioning the triangles as shown.

5. Sew band B to the short side of each of the units from Step 4.

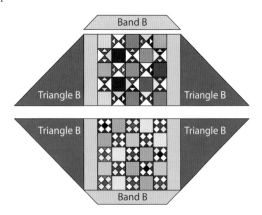

6. Sew a band C to the top and bottom of the Evening Star Compass unit.

7. Sew the remaining band B's to the opposite ends of the unit.

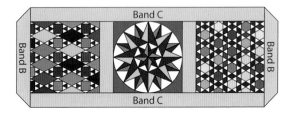

8. Sew a triangle A to each of the band B's and join the 3 units together into a square.

9. Add band D to the sides of the center unit and band E to the top and bottom. Sew a side border to each side of the center unit.

10. Sew the top and bottom borders in place, adding band F to the top and bottom. Sew band G to the sides to complete the quilt top.

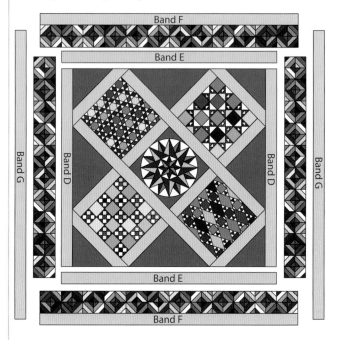

PORTICO PAVEMENT

Portico Pavement, 78" × 84", by Norah McMeeking and the Bella Brigade, quilted by Kim Peterson of Kimberwood Quilting

Take the simple idea behind this design and make a strong statement that will suit even the most urban décor. In fact, you could use decorator fabric in the center if you wish. The bands are wide enough to hold an appliqué vine. You'll need determination to sew the pieced outermost border, but it certainly has a wow factor—and libraries have great audio books to while away the "pieceful" hours.

Before you begin, consider how you might vary this design:

- Replace the outermost border with an elaborate appliqué vine.
- Place a solid band in the center of the outermost border.
- Use the border to frame a wholecloth quilt.

Because this quilt uses both 6"- and 9"-wide borders, it will take a little extra thought to alter the design of the 9" border. It would be easy to change the 9" border to any 6" block or to blocks that build to 12" wide for a different sized finished quilt. Though I encourage you to do your own thing with this design, the following describes how I made *Portico Pavement*.

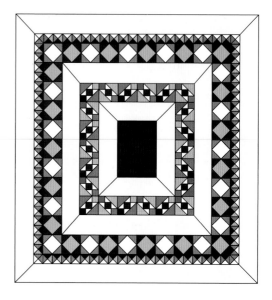

Fabrics and Cutting Requirements

Backing and binding: 8 yards

Batting: 86″ × 92″

CENTER VARIABLE STAR

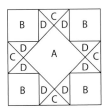

Make 6 blocks
6″ × 6″ finished

PATCH		FABRIC	CUTTING SIZE	QUANTITY	TOTAL PATCHES
A	□	Scraps of gold and dark yellow	4″ × 4″	6	6
B	□	⅓ yard mixed dark blue	3″ × 3″	24	24
C	⊠		4″ × 4″	6	24
D	⊠	¼ yard mixed light	4″ × 4″	12	48

POISED SQUARE-IN-A-SQUARE MIDDLE BORDER

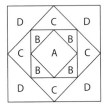

Make 22 blocks 6″ × 6″ finished.

PATCH		FABRIC	CUTTING SIZE	QUANTITY	TOTAL PATCHES
A	□	¼ yard mixed light	3″ × 3″	22	22
B	⊠	⅜ yard mixed dark	4¼″ × 4¼″	22	88
C	⊠	⅝ yard mixed light	5″ × 5″	22	88
D	◻	1 yard mixed dark	4¾″ × 4¾″	44	88

PORTICO OUTER BORDER

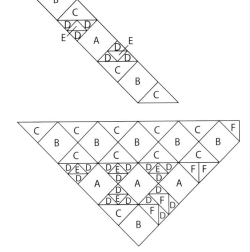

PATCH		FABRIC*	CUTTING SIZE	QUANTITY	TOTAL PATCHES
A	□	⅝ yard mixed medium blues	3″ × 3″	80	80
B	□	1⅛ yards mixed yellows	3″ × 3″	160	160
C	⊠	1½ yards mixed dark blues	5″ × 5″	78	312
D	⊠	1⅛ yards mixed lights	3½″ × 3½″	118	472
E	⊠	½ yard mixed medium blues	3½″ × 3½″	38	152
F	◻	Medium and dark blue scraps and a pale scrap	3″ × 3″	2 pale, 2 medium blue, 8 dark blue	24: 4 pale, 4 medium blue, 16 dark blue

BANDS

BAND*	FABRIC	CUTTING SIZE	QUANTITY
A	3 yards pale blue	6½" × 12½"	2
B		6½" × 30½"	2
C		6½" × 36½"	2
D		6½" × 54½"	2
E		6½" × 66½"	2
F		6½" × 84½"	2

* Cut all bands on length of grain.

Note

I know quilt judges would like to see mitered borders in this quilt, but butted joins are more faithful to the floors' stonework. Mitering is certainly a choice you can make.

Paper Foundations

Read General Instructions (pages 17–27) before starting.

Note

CAUTION

Remember that stitching lines are on what will be the *wrong side* of the completed block. Keep that reversal in mind when color placement varies or blocks have a direction (such as the border filler sections).

Foundation Piecing

VARIABLE STAR CENTER

1. Trace or copy 6 foundations from pattern pullout page P2.

2. Piece in numbered order.

3. There are 4 sections in this block. Join section a to section b, pressing the seam allowance toward section b. Foundation piece section c, making 2 per block. When you join the sections together, the seams will marry.

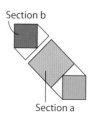
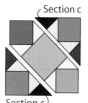

4. Join the completed blocks in 2 rows of 3 blocks each. Join the rows to complete the center unit.

POISED SQUARE-IN-A-SQUARE MIDDLE BORDER

1. Trace or copy 22 foundations from pattern pullout page P1.

2. Piece in numbered order.

3. Sew the blocks into 2 rows of 4 blocks and 2 rows of 7 blocks.

Top/bottom rows

Side rows

Make 2 of each row.

Note

Do not trim before joining, but use the wider seam allowance to aid in pressing *seams open*. After pressing, carefully trim the seam allowance to ¼", using the edge of the foundation as a guide.

PORTICO PAVEMENT OUTER BORDER

This border uses foundations with sections that join in diagonal rows. This allows most of the seams to marry, resulting in beautiful matches. Sections a, b, and c make up each row. Simply rotate alternate rows to allow the seams to marry.

1. Trace or copy 68 Portico Border foundations on pattern pullout page P2.

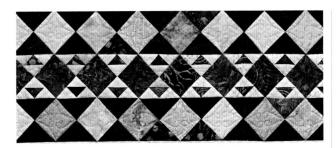

Tip

You'll get more sparkle if you keep the values and colors the same but mix up the prints. Good contrast will make the middle section stand out.

2. Label at least a few foundations for color placement and chain sew the sections to speed up the process.

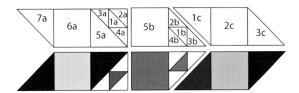

3. Join sections a, b, and c to make diagonal strips.

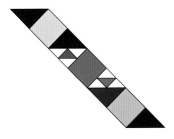

4. Make 2 of each border: Join 18 rows of border strips for the 2 longer borders, and join 16 rows for the 2 shorter borders.

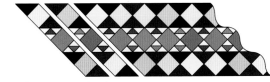

Piecing the outermost border

Portico Border Filler Section

1. Trace or copy 4 foundations from pattern pullout page P2.

2. Piece in numbered order.

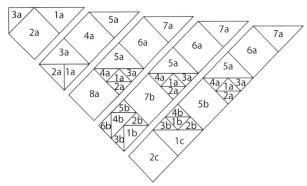

Note

Remember that the color diagrams show the front of the unit, while the foundations are the back.

3. Join the rows together to complete 4 filler units.

Make 4 of each.

4. Add a filler unit to one end of each border. Note that you will attach the border filler to the same side of each border, so the border filler wraps around the corner.

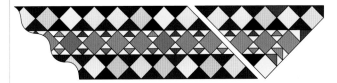

5. Trim border units, adding a ¼″ seam allowance using the foundation edges as a guide. Carefully remove the papers.

Quilt Assembly

This quilt top assembles medallion style, from the center out.

1. Sew band A to the top and bottom of the center unit. Add band B to each side.

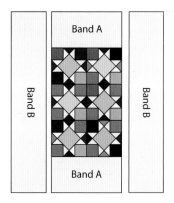

Tip

When joining a pieced unit to a plain band (or a setting triangle or square, and so on), use a quilter's ruler to make small tick marks on the bands where the main seams of the units should touch—in this case, every 6″ on the inside edge of the band and every 6″ on the outside too. Remember to allow a ¼″ seam allowance at the corner edges. Line up the seams with the tick marks.

Pin by matching seams to the tick marks on the plain fabric.

2. Sew the short rows of the middle border to the top and bottom edges; then add the longer rows to the sides.

3. Sew band C to the top and bottom of the quilt and band D to the sides.

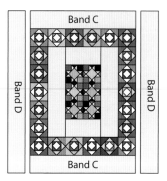

4. *Now the tricky part:* Find the dark blue F triangles, which you set aside when you cut all those patches for the outer borders. These 4 triangles are cut to size, including seam allowance.

5. Sew the triangles to the corners of bands D as diagrammed, using a very tiny *partial seam.*

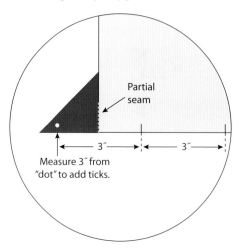

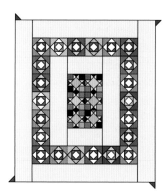

6. Add tick marks to the outside edge of each band C, starting at the dot on the triangle. Make a tick mark every 3″ to indicate where the seams of the pieced border meet the band.

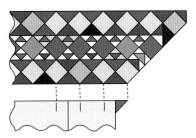

7. Beginning at the dot on triangle F, sew the top and bottom borders to the bands. Leave the last 6″ of each border unsewn (a partial seam).

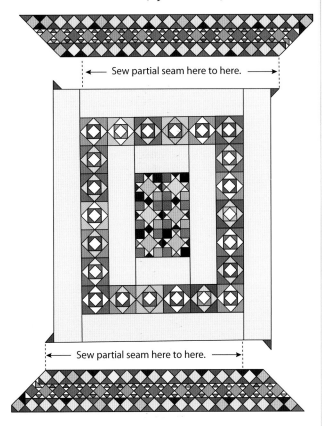

8. Add the side borders.

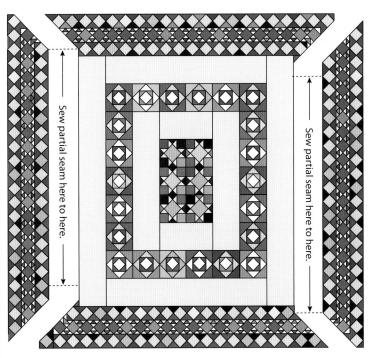

9. Carefully match and pin the diagonal edges of the border together. Sew the diagonal seam, *stopping at the dot at the inside corner.*

10. Complete the remaining partial seams at the corners, again stopping at the dot.

11. To complete the quilt top, add band E to the top and bottom and band F to the sides.

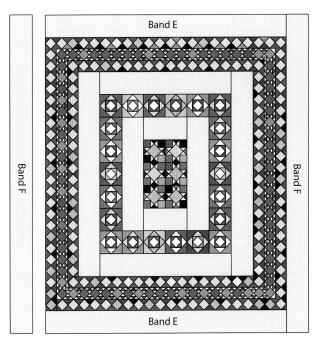

ORVIETO SAMPLER

Orvieto Sampler, 83″ × 83″, by Norah McMeeking and the Bella Brigade, quilted by Kim Peterson of Kimberwood Quilting

Standing in the piazza in front of Orvieto's cathedral one autumn morning, I saw it bathed in sunlight, its complexion famously pink. The façade is covered with exquisite Cosmati-esque work in hundreds of tiny borders and ribbons of mosaic wrapped around pillars. Considered a masterpiece of Italian Gothic architecture, the duomo, begun in 1290, took more than a century to complete.

As with all the quilts in this book, there are many ways to vary this design. Before you begin, think about the possibilities:

- Combine appliqué, patchwork, and plain units.
- Fill the half-medallions with a beautiful print.
- Make a puzzle quilt by using the same patchwork units but varying the fabric placement.

This quilt is made with 9 units, each 15" square, so Salerno Sampler blocks could be mixed with these. Each square could be made of 25 blocks, 3" × 3", or 9 blocks, 5" × 5". Look through the pattern pullouts at the back of the book and choose the blocks *you* like the most. Though I encourage you to do your own thing with this design, the following describes how I made *Orvieto Sampler*.

Fabric and Cutting Requirements

Backing and binding: 7¼ yards

Background: 1⅞ yards burgundy print

Cut background using template on pattern pullout page P3.

Batting: 91″ × 91″

DOUBLE COSMATI TRIANGLES

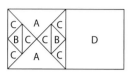

Make 12 pieced blocks and 13 alternate plain blocks, each 3″ × 3″ finished.

PATCH		FABRIC	CUTTING SIZE	QUANTITY	TOTAL PATCHES
A	⊠	¼ yard batik	5″ × 5″	6	24
B	⊠	⅛ yard mixed darks and brights	3½″ × 3½″	6	24
C	⊠	¼ yard mixed lights	3½″ × 3½″	18	72
D	☐	Scraps: 4 gold, 4 rose, 5 plum	4″ × 4″	13	13

COSMATI REFLECTIONS

Make 12 pieced blocks and 13 plain blocks, each 3″ × 3″ finished.

PATCH		FABRIC	CUTTING SIZE	QUANTITY	TOTAL PATCHES
A	◺	¼ yard mixed darks and mediums	3″ × 3″	24	48
B	◺	¼ yard mixed lights	3″ × 3″	24	48
C	☐	Scraps: 4 gold, 2 plum, 2 rose, 2 pink, 3 batik	4″ × 4″	13	13

COSMATI KALEIDOSCOPE

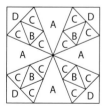

Make 9 blocks 5″ × 5″ finished.

PATCH		FABRIC	CUTTING SIZE	QUANTITY*	TOTAL PATCHES
A	CT	⅜ yard assorted pinks	3½″ strips	2 strips	36
B	CT	¼ yard rose and plum	2¼″ strips	2 strips	36
C	CT	⅓ yard light	2¼″ strips	4 strips	108
D	◺	¼ yard rose and plum	3″ × 3″	18	36

Quantity depends on number of colors/fabrics used.

TRIP TO ROME

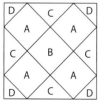

Make 9 blocks 5″ × 5″ finished.

PATCH		FABRIC	CUTTING SIZE	QUANTITY	TOTAL PATCHES
A	☐	⅜ yard mixed lights and darks	2¾″ × 2¾″	36	36
B	☐	Mixed medium and dark scraps	2¾″ × 2¾″	9	9
C	⊠	Mixed light and dark scraps	4½″ × 4½″	4 lights, 5 darks	36
D	◺	Mixed light and dark scraps	2¾″ × 2¾″	8 lights, 10 darks	36

CHAPEL
Block I

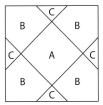

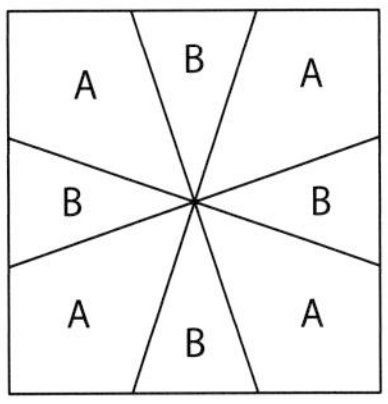

Make 4 blocks
5″ × 5″ finished.

PATCH		FABRIC	CUTTING SIZE	QUANTITY	TOTAL PATCHES
A	CT	⅓ yard batik	4″ strip	2 strips	16
B	CT	¼ yard ivory	4″ strip	1 strip	16

Block II

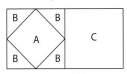

Make 5 blocks
5″ × 5″ finished.

PATCH		FABRIC	CUTTING SIZE	QUANTITY	TOTAL PATCHES
A	☐	⅛ yard orange	3¼″ × 3¼″	5	5
B	CT	¼ yard plum	3½″ strip	2 strips	20
C	⊠	Yellow scraps	3¼″ × 3¼″	5	20

POISED SQUARE-IN-A-SQUARE

Make 48 pieced blocks and
52 alternate plain blocks,
each 3″ × 3″ finished.

PATCH		FABRIC	CUTTING SIZE	QUANTITY	TOTAL PATCHES
A	☐	⅜ yard mixed lights	3″ × 3″	48	48
B	◹	¾ yard mixed darks and mediums	3″ × 3″	96	192
C	☐	¾ yard batik	4″ × 4″	52	52

PALATINE HALF-MEDALLIONS

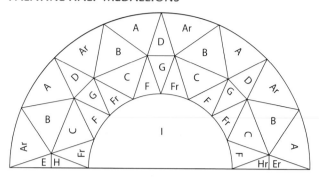

PATCH		FABRIC	CUTTING SIZE	QUANTITY	TOTAL PATCHES
A and Ar	CT	⅜ yard plum	4" × WOF	3 strips	16 A, 16 Ar
B	CT	¼ yard light green batik	4" × WOF	2 strips	16
C	CT	¼ yard batik	4" × WOF	1 strip	16
D, E , Er, F, and Fr	CT	⅜ yard yellow	4" × WOF	3 strips	12 D, 4 each E and Er, 16 each F and Fr
G, H, and Hr	CT	⅛" yard batik print	4" × WOF	1 strip	12 G, 4 each H and Hr
I	CT	9" × 18" coral strip	4½" × 9"	4	4

BANDS

*N*ote

I chose to assemble this top with partial seams so I could enhance the appearance of interweaving. If you don't like that method or don't need it, simply adjust the cutting sizes of the bands as you would for normal sashing strips.

BAND*	FABRIC	CUTTING SIZE	QUANTITY
A	4⅛ yards	4½" × 34½"	4
B		4½" × 34⅞"	4
C		4½" × 15⅞"	4
D		4½" × 19½"	4
E CT			4
F		4½" × 75½"	2
G		4½" × 83½"	2

* Cut all bands on length of grain, except E, which uses a cutting template.

Paper Foundations

Read General Instructions (pages 17–27) before starting.

*N*ote

CAUTION

Remember that stitching lines are on what will be the *wrong side* of the completed block. Keep that reversal in mind when color placement varies or blocks have a direction (like Cosmati Reflections).

Foundation Piecing

DOUBLE COSMATI TRIANGLES

1. There are 2 foundations provided on pullout page P2, because the triangles change direction in alternate rows. Trace or copy 12 foundations—6 containing patch 6c and 6 containing patch 6a. Cut patch 6a off 2 of them.

2. Take the 6 foundations containing patch 6c and piece in numbered order, placing gold and plum alternate blocks as shown. Join the blocks to create rows.

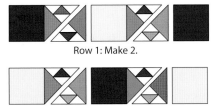

Row 1: Make 2.

Row 1 with color of plain blocks reversed: Make 1.

3. Take the 6 foundations containing patch 6a and piece in numbered order, using rose for the alternate plain blocks. Join the blocks to create rows.

Row 2: Make 2.

4. Join the rows to complete the unit.

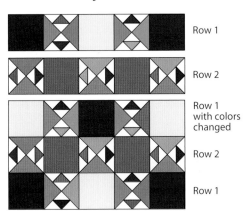

Row 1

Row 2

Row 1 with colors changed

Row 2

Row 1

COSMATI REFLECTIONS

1. Trace or copy 13 foundations from pattern pullout page P1. Remove patch 5a from 3 of them.

2. Foundation piece sections a and b in numbered order, using the following illustrations to guide color placement of the light/dark triangles and the plain squares.

3. Join sections into rows.

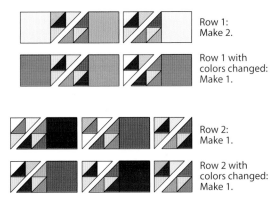

Row 1: Make 2.

Row 1 with colors changed: Make 1.

Row 2: Make 1.

Row 2 with colors changed: Make 1.

4. Join the rows.

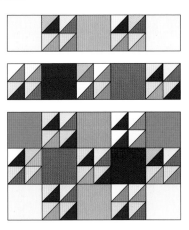

COSMATI KALEIDOSCOPE

1. Trace or copy 9 foundations from pattern pullout page P2.

2. Each block has 4 sections, 2 of section a and 2 of section b. Join in pairs, pressing the seam allowance in the same direction on both.

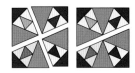

Note

Be sure the center match is correct at the end of this step. The center won't be perfect if it's off at this stage.

3. Join the pairs of sections into blocks. The seams should marry when the sections are placed right sides together. Press all the seams in the same direction around the center. Unpick a few stitches at the middle to free the seam allowance when necessary.

4. Join the blocks into rows of 3 and the rows to each other to complete the unit.

TRIP TO ROME

1. Trace or copy 9 foundations from pattern pullout page P4.

2. This block has 3 sections. Follow the piecing sequence on the foundations so the seams will marry. Piece 5 blocks in numbered order with dark values in the triangles and light values for squares. Piece 4 blocks with light values in those triangles and dark values for the squares. Join the sections.

3. Join the blocks into rows of 3, alternating dark and light triangles as shown. Join the rows to each other to complete the unit.

CHAPEL BLOCKS

This design is made of two blocks, set in alternating rows.

Chapel Block I

1. Trace or copy 4 foundations from pattern pullout page P4.

2. Each block has 2 sections. Piece in numbered order. The seams will marry. Join 2 sections to make each block.

Chapel Block II

1. Trace or copy 5 foundations from pattern pullout page P4.

2. Each block has 3 sections. Piece in numbered order. The seams will marry. Join 3 sections to make each block.

3. Join blocks I and II in rows. Join the rows to complete the unit.

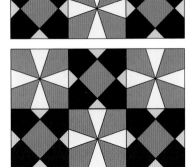

POISED SQUARE-IN-A-SQUARE

1. Trace or copy 52 foundations from pattern pullout page P1. Cut 12 of them in half. Discard 4 of the poised square foundations.

2. Piece each block in numbered order.

3. Join into rows. Trim the 12 precut patches to 3½″ × 3½″ to add to the rows that need them.

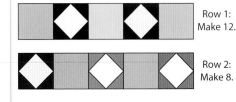

Row 1: Make 12.

Row 2: Make 8.

4. Join the 5 rows to complete a unit. Repeat this step to make a total of 4 units.

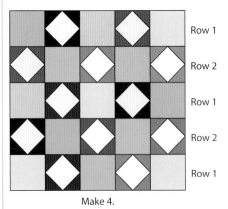

Row 1
Row 2
Row 1
Row 2
Row 1

Make 4.

PALATINE HALF-MEDALLIONS

1. Trace or copy 4 foundations from pattern pullout page P3.

2. Make freezer-paper cutting templates as described in Using Cutting Templates (page 18) and use them to cut all the patches required for the 4 half-medallions.

3. Piece sections a through d in numbered order.

4. Join sections a and b in pairs, as shown.

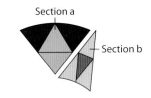

Section a

Section b

5. Join 3 a/b pairs as shown. Add a section c at the left end of the arc. Add a section a to the right and then a section d to complete the unit. Repeat to make 4 half-medallions. *Do not trim yet.*

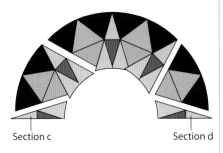

Section c   Section d

6. Trace or copy the inner half-circle pattern on pattern pullout page P3, 4 times onto freezer paper. Glue the curved seam allowance to the back of the template, easing in a curve. Use basting glue to hold the half-circle in position on the half-medallion. Machine appliqué into place. Trim seam allowances.

Medallion Corners

TEMPLATES

1. Trace the pattern on pattern pullout page P3 for the curved band E. Read Making Foundations (page 19) for directions on making duplicate templates.

2. Make 4 accurate freezer paper templates.

3. Carefully trace the background template on pattern pullout page P3 twice onto freezer paper and once onto tracing paper. Reverse the tracing-paper drawing, and from it carefully trace 2 reversed versions of the template.

4. Cut out the freezer-paper templates carefully and join together to make a 4-part template for the corner background, as diagrammed on pullout page P3. Repeat for the 3 remaining corners, or reuse the template you've just made.

CUTTING THE CURVED BANDS

1. Iron the curved band E freezer-paper templates to the wrong side of the band fabric.

2. Mark the seamline along the curved edges, including the tick marks. Cut out, adding a ¼″ seam allowance on all sides.

3. Leave the templates in place until you're ready to join the medallions and corners.

MARKING AND CUTTING THE BACKGROUND

1. Iron the background template, or templates, to the wrong side of the background fabric so the corner is on grain. Leave room to add a ¼″ seam allowance.

2. Mark a stitching line along the curved edge of the freezer paper, adding tick marks to the seam allowance.

3. Using the edge of the template as a guide, add a ¼″ seam allowance to the straight sides as you cut out the fabric. Cut ¼″ away from the curve, adding the seam allowance.

4. Once the corner piece is trimmed and the curve marked, you can remove and reuse the template to cut another corner.

TRIMMING BANDS B AND C

Use the 45° line on a quilter's ruler to trim off the corner on bands B and C at the angle shown here. Trim precisely into the corner. The bands are shown right side up.

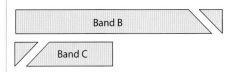

CORNER ASSEMBLY

Read the important information in Pinning and Sewing Curves (page 25).

1. Remove the template from the curved band and sew it to a half-medallion. Sew with the band on the top.

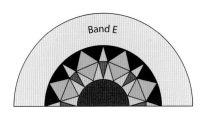

Band E

2. Iron the background template to the wrong side of the fabric. Cut out, adding ¼" seam allowance. Use the edge of the template to mark the curved stitching line and ticks. Remove and reuse the template. Sew the band to the curved corner background, matching tick marks and sewing with the background fabric on top.

Press the seam allowances toward the band in all cases.

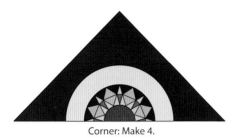

Corner: Make 4.

3. Make 4 corner units.

Quilt Assembly

1. To attach the bands accurately, make tick marks as described in Matching Bands to Quilt Units (page 26). Adjust the measurements for each patchwork variation.

2. Add a band C, *angles positioned as shown*, to the Cosmati Kaleidoscope, Double Cosmati Triangle, Cosmati Reflections, and Trip to Rome units. Add band D to the right edge of each patchwork variation, as shown.

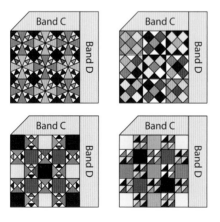

3. Sew band B to each Poised Square-in-a-Square unit, using a partial seam ending at the red dot, as shown in the diagram. Join a patchwork variation to each of the Poised Square-in-a-Square units, as shown.

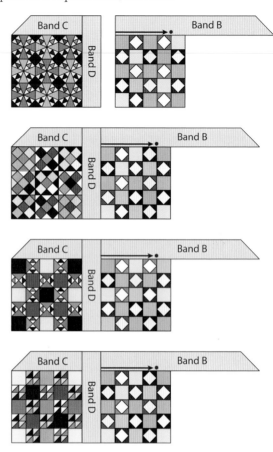

4. Sew a band A to each side of the Chapel Blocks unit, using partial seams, starting with seam 1 and sewing in the direction shown, as you work your way around the Chapel Blocks unit.

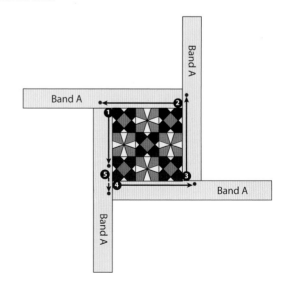

5. Join units to the top and bottom of the quilt center, with full seams (A). Then, complete partial seams 1 and 3.

6. Repeat Step 5 with the remaining 2 units to complete the center of the quilt.

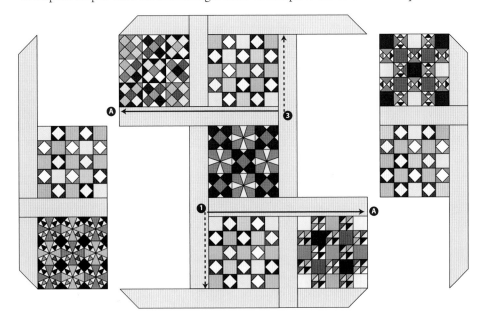

7. Add a completed corner unit to each side of the center.

8. Complete the quilt top by sewing band F to the sides and band G to the top and bottom.

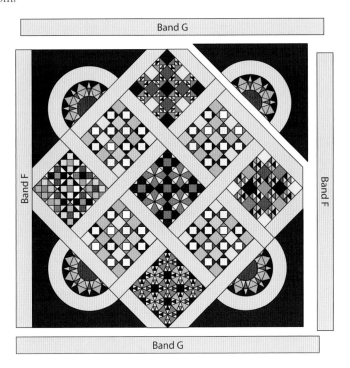

SAN CLEMENTE BORDERS

San Clemente Borders, 90" × 90", by Norah McMeeking, quilted by Dee Angus of Tomorrow's Treasures

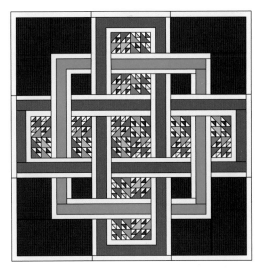

Many of the smallest-scale Cosmati designs that decorate pillars, lintels, and baptismal fonts use interlaced shapes. This quilt's design comes from an altar frontal. The patchwork is based on 4″ blocks.

Before beginning, consider varying the design in one of these ways:

- Substitute whole pieces of large-scale prints for the patchwork borders and put appliqué in the inner squares and rectangles.

- Put patchwork or a compass in the center square.

- Use easy-to-foundation-piece Flying Geese blocks in all the interlacing borders.

The instructions describe how I made *San Clemente Borders*. This quilt uses partial seams for assembly—easier to do than to diagram, so don't let all the labels discourage you!

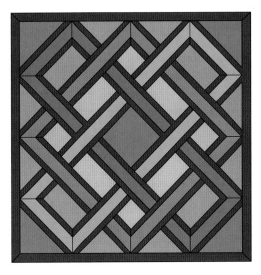

These interlacing borders are based on 4″ × 4″ blocks, and you can substitute any 4″ block in place of the ones in the sample. Be aware that some blocks are cut in half by the interlacing and will be 2″ × 4″. Though I encourage you to do your own thing with this design, the following describes how I made *San Clemente Borders*.

Fabrics and Cutting Requirements

Backing and binding: 8½ yards

Batting: 98″ × 98″

TURNING TRIANGLES BORDER

4″ × 4″ finished

PATCH		FABRIC	CUTTING SIZE	QUANTITY	TOTAL PATCHES
A	⊠	¾ yard mixed mediums and darks	6″ × 6″	23	92 (88 for full blocks, 4 for half-blocks)
B	⊠	¾ yard background print	6″ × 6″	23	92 (88 for full blocks, 4 for half-blocks)
C	◻	Background print scraps for 4; mixed medium and dark scraps for 4	3½″ × 3½″	8	16 (for half-blocks)

PALIO PENNANT BORDER

4″ × 4″ finished

PATCH		FABRIC	CUTTING SIZE	QUANTITY	TOTAL PATCHES
A and Ar	CT	1⅛ yards mixed mediums and darks	5″ × WOF	5 strips	50 each of A and Ar (46 for full blocks, 4 for half-blocks)
B	CT		3″ × WOF	2 strips	48 (46 for full blocks, 2 for half-blocks)
C	CT	⅝ yard background	3″ × WOF	6 strips	144 (138 for blocks, 6 for half-blocks)

COSMATI TRIANGLE BORDER

4″ × 4″ finished

PATCH		FABRIC	CUTTING SIZE	QUANTITY	TOTAL PATCHES
A	◻	1⅛ yards mixed mediums and darks	5½″ × 5½″	24	48 (44 for full blocks, 4 for half-blocks)
B	◻		3½″ × 3½″	26	52 (44 for full blocks, 8 for half-blocks)
C	◻	⅞ yard background	3½″ × 3½″	72	144 (132 for full blocks, 12 for half-blocks)

SETTING SQUARES, RECTANGLES, AND TRIANGLES

PATCH		FABRIC	CUTTING SIZE	QUANTITY	TOTAL PATCHES
A	☐	1 yard print #1	16½″ × 16½″	1	1
B	☐		8½″ × 8½″	4	4
C	▭		8½″ × 16½″	4	4
D	▭	⅝ yards print #2	8½″ × 16½″	4	4
E	⊠	2⅞ yards solid-reading print	23¾″ × 23¾″	2	8
F	◻		23½″ × 23½″	2	4

BANDS

BAND*	FABRIC	CUTTING SIZE	QUANTITY
A and D	2½ yards cream	2½″ × 32½″	16
B		2½″ × 26½″	4
C		2½″ × 30½″	4
E		2½″ × 10½″	8
F		2½″ × 14½″	8
G		2½″ × 40½″	4
H		2½″ × 16½″	4

Cut all bands on length of grain.

Paper Foundations

Read General Instructions (pages 17–27) before starting.

CAUTION

Remember that stitching lines are on what will be the *wrong side* of the completed block. Keep that reversal in mind because all the blocks in this project have a direction. You'll also need to be careful with each block's orientation as you create the borders.

Foundation Piecing

TURNING TRIANGLES BORDER

This border is assembled on the diagonal, and section a is rotated every other row, which allows the seams to marry and also creates the "turning" effect.

1. Trace or copy 36 section a foundations, 8 section b foundations, and 8 section c foundations from pattern pullout page P5.

2. Sew sections in the quantities shown. Foundation piece in the numbered order so the seams will marry. Label the foundations for fabric placement as necessary for each border unit.

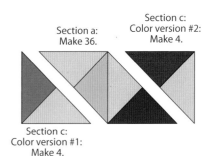

Section a:
Make 36.

Section c:
Color version #2:
Make 4.

Section c:
Color version #1:
Make 4.

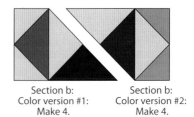

Section b:
Color version #1:
Make 4.

Section b:
Color version #2:
Make 4.

3. Join the sections into rows; make 2 of each.

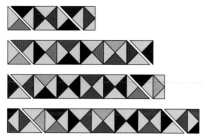

Make 2 of each.

PALIO PENNANT BORDER

This border is made of 3 sections.

1. Trace or copy 46 full block foundations from pattern pullout page P5. Trace or copy foundations for the partial blocks: 2 each of section c and section d.

2. Make sections in the quantities shown below. Foundation piece in the numbered order so the seams will marry. Label the foundations for fabric placement as necessary for each border unit.

Section a: Section d: Section c:
Make 46.   Make 2.   Make 2.

3. Join the sections into rows. Note the blocks that are rotated. Make 2 of each.

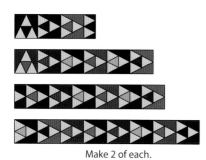

Make 2 of each.

COSMATI TRIANGLE BORDER

This border is made of 5 different sections.

1. Trace or copy 44 section a foundations from pattern pullout page P7. Also trace or copy foundations for the partial blocks: 2 each of section c, cr, d, and dr.

2. Make sections in the quantities shown below. Foundation piece in the numbered order. Label the foundations for fabric placement as necessary for each border unit.

Section a: Section d: Section dr:
Make 44.   Make 2.   Make 2.

Section c: Section cr:
Make 2.   Make 2.

3. Join the sections into rows; make 1 of each, as shown below.

Pay close attention to the orientation of the triangles if you want them all to point the same direction in the finished quilt.

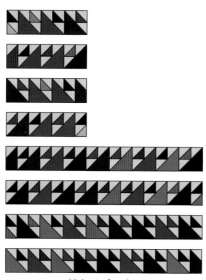

Make 1 of each.

Quilt Assembly

Now the fun begins! You'll be using a lot of partial seams to build this design. If you're not used to working with these, they're just a start/stop way of avoiding set-in corners. Sort the units by block design and label the bands.

Tip

You'll find it very helpful to mark on the wrong side of each band where the pieced borders' seams are supposed to meet the seam allowance. Remember to begin with the ¼" seam allowance. If you make a mark every 2" after that, you'll be in clover. You won't use some of them, but you won't have to keep count when you mark this particular design.

Follow the diagrams carefully. Using partial seams is a start/stop process, a little messy but easy to do. If you have the space, it's a good idea to arrange the design as you want it to look when finished. Work in sections as follows.

1. Join border units and bands that have a single complete seam.

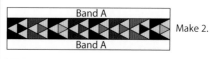

Make 2.

Make 2.

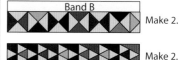

Make 2.

Make 2.

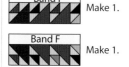

Make 1.

Make 1.

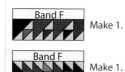

Make 1.

Make 1.

2. Join setting pieces and bands that have complete seams. Sew band H to setting rectangle C; add band E. *It's very important to sew the band to the correct edge of the unit.* Make 4.

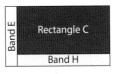

Make 4.

3. Sew band A to the bias edge of triangle F. Make 4.

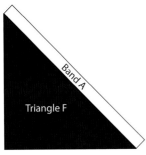

Make 4.

Note

The following units use partial seams—that is, seams that begin by joining the edges of two units but stop short, leaving the last 2″–3″ unstitched. You need some loose space to maneuver the fabric when you eventually finish the seams.

4. Follow the diagram to sew the center unit. Start with a partial seam to add the Turning Triangles unit, beginning at the corner of square A and working counterclockwise. Stop before you get to the adjacent corner. Most of the patchwork will be hanging loose.

5. Add the Palio Pennant unit to the top of square A. Again, go counterclockwise around the center. Stop partway across the Turning Triangles / squares unit, leaving about 3″ free. Repeat on the 2 remaining sides, adding a Turning Triangles unit and then another Palio Pennant unit.

6. Now find the end of the first seam and, overlapping the stitching, sew about 7″ further, as shown by the dashed line, still leaving a partial seam. Set the unit aside briefly.

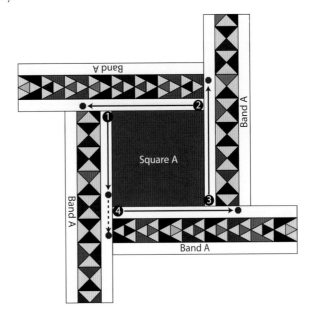

7. Add rectangle D to the band B units, positioning as shown. Start the seam at the outside edge of the rectangle. Sew about 5″ and stop, leaving about 3″ of the rectangle unattached.

8. Make 2 of each unit shown.

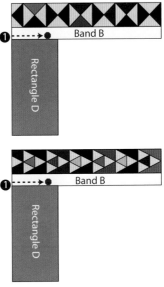

Make 2 of each.

9. Add the units just completed to the center. Sew seams in the order shown in the diagram. Sew a rectangle D / Palio Pennant unit to the center with a partial seam, and then continue the partial seam shown at #2. Work your way around the center, adding a Turning Triangles unit next and then the others in turn.

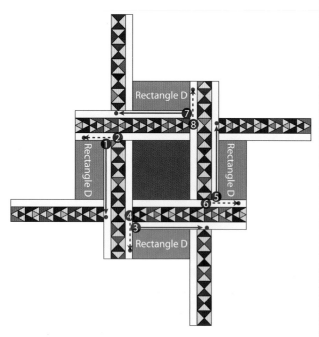

10. Set the center unit aside.

ASSEMBLE INNER CORNER UNITS

Next, you'll create units needed to set the quilt center on point, and build out toward the corners. Refer to the assembly diagram in Step 9 (at right) as you sew the seams in numbered order.

1. Sew band A to square B with seam 1, a partial seam.

2. Add band E with a complete seam.

3. Sew band C to square B opposite band A with seam 3, a partial seam.

4. Add a Cosmati triangle border that is 8½ blocks long to band A with seam 4, a complete seam. Make sure the triangles point in the direction shown in the diagrams.

5. Add a 3½-block Cosmati triangle border with seam 5, making sure it matches the orientation of the longer border. *Be careful about orientation—they're all different!*

6. Sew band G to the unit with seam 6, a complete seam.

7. Sew triangle E to band F with seam 7, a complete seam.

8. Attach the other side of the triangle by continuing the partial seam to within 3″ of the point of the triangle with seam 8, keeping it still a partial seam.

9. Make a total of 4 units. Each unit needs a different orientation for the Cosmati Triangle borders; matching the orientation at Step 5 will produce each variation. *Watch the orientation of those Cosmati Triangle border units!*

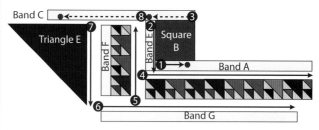

Assembly diagram shows seams in sewing order.

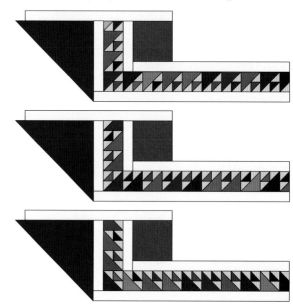

10. Sew seams in numbered order to attach each Cosmati Triangle unit to the center. You'll feel like you're in the arms of an octopus, but be patient—you're almost there. Repeat seaming steps with all 4 units, *being careful to keep the Cosmati Triangle units in their correct positions.*

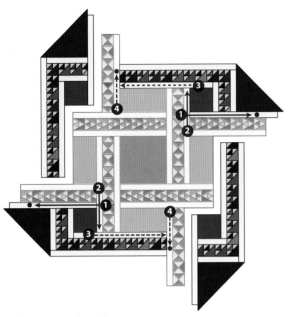

Adding units to the quilt center

ADD CORNER UNITS

Now you'll make the corner units, then add them to the quilt top. The diagrams show seams numbered by sewing order.

1. To make each corner, start with the rectangle C unit. Add the 6-block Turning Triangle border, then the 3½-block border. Add triangle F and then triangle E to complete the corner.

2. Repeat Step 1 to make a second Turning Triangle corner unit.

3. Repeat Steps 1 and 2 with the remaining rectangle C units and the Palio Pennant units.

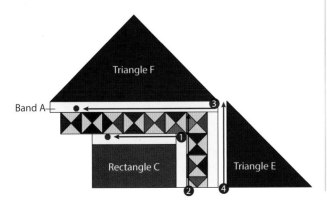

4. Add the corners to the center. First sew the rectangle unit with a long seam to the edge of the quilt. Then sew a series of short seams to complete the remaining partial seams following the numbered seams in the diagram.

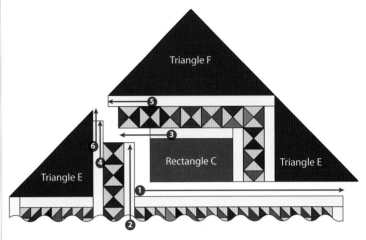

Corner assembly diagram

SICILY SOUVENIR

Sicily Souvenir, 66" x 84", by Norah McMeeking and the Bella Brigade, quilted by Kim Peterson of Kimberwood Quilting

The elements of this design originate in the thousands of motifs in the Palatine Chapel, Palermo, Sicily. This World Heritage Site was built in the twelfth century by a Norman king, and every inch of it displays patterns from Christian, Hebrew, and Islamic traditions. Volcanic Mount Etna shares the island and inspired my color choices.

Before you begin, think of how you might vary this design:

- Substitute any 6″ block in the border.
- Make all the medallions match or put a large one in the center as well.
- Add embroidery to make the bands seem to weave.
- Appliqué something gorgeous in the medallions in place of the piecing.

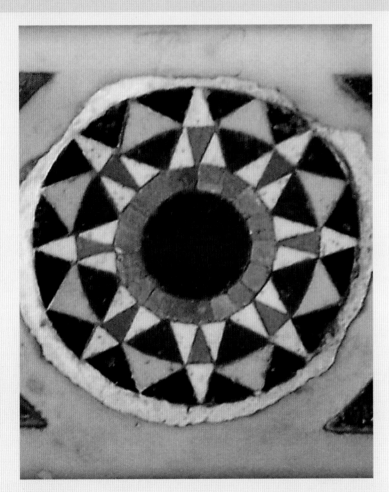

Because the center square measures 21″ × 21,″ substitution choices are limited to only other 3″ blocks with 1″ sashing (if you want to work with full inch measurements). The 6″ border could be replaced by two rows of 3″ blocks or three rows of 2″ blocks. Though I encourage you to do your own thing with this design, the following describes how I made *Sicily Souvenir*.

Fabric and Cutting Requirements

Backing and binding: 5½ yards

Batting: 74″ × 92″

TIBER PAVEMENT CENTER SQUARE

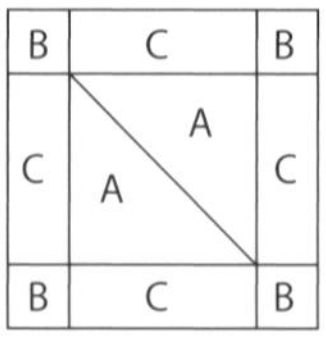

21″ × 21″ finished, with
3″ and 1″ patches

PATCH		FABRIC	CUTTING SIZE	QUANTITY	TOTAL PATCHES
A	◻	Mixed dark, medium, and light neutrals totaling ⅜ yard	4½″ × 4½″	25	50
B	☐	Mixed blacks totaling ⅛ yard	1¾″ × 1¾″	36	36
C	▭	Mixed tans totaling ½ yard	1¾″ × 3¾″	60	60

MEDALLIONS

Heritage medallion, 15″ diameter

Elinor medallion, 15″ diameter

Norman medallion, 15″ diameter

Palatine medallion, 15″ diameter

Make foundations from the masters on pattern pullout pages P5–P8 for each medallion and use them to make cutting templates as described in General Instructions (pages 17–27). Use scraps totaling about 1½ yards from the borders and center units, supplemented with coordinating fat quarters as you wish. See the following foundation piecing instructions for fabric colors and quantities for each medallion.

SICILIAN BORDER

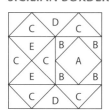

6″ × 6″ finished

PATCH		FABRIC	CUTTING SIZE	QUANTITY	TOTAL PATCHES
A	☐	Light tan scraps totaling ⅜ yard	3″ × 3″	42	42
B	◻	Black scraps totaling ¾ yard	3″ × 3″	84	168
C	⊠	Mixed light scraps totaling 1⅛ yards	4½″ × 4½″	63	252
D	⊠	Taupe/olive scraps totaling ⅞ yard	4½″ × 4½″	42	168
E	⊠	Medium grays and tans totaling ½ yard	4½″ × 4½″	21	84

BANDS

BAND*	FABRIC	CUTTING SIZE	QUANTITY
A	3⅝ yards cream or white	3½" × 21½"	2
B		3½" × 27½"	2
C		3½" × 48½"	2
D		3½" × 60½"	2
E		3½" × 78½"	2
F		3½" × 66½"	2
G **CT**			16

* Cut bands A–F on length of grain.

BACKGROUND

BACKGROUND		FABRIC	CUTTING SIZE	QUANTITY
Half-square setting triangles	◻	2 yards beige	32⅞" × 32⅞"	2
Background setting pieces	T			2

Paper Foundations

Read General Instructions (pages 17–27) before starting.

CAUTION

Remember that stitching lines are on what will be the *wrong side* of the completed block. Keep that reversal in mind when color placement varies or blocks have a direction (such as the Sicily Border blocks).

Foundation Piecing

TIBER PAVEMENT CENTER

1. Trace or copy 3 section a foundations, 2 section b foundations, and 6 section c foundations from pattern pullout page P3.

2. Piece in numbered order using random color placement for the triangles.

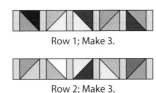

Row 1; Make 3.

Row 2; Make 3.

3. Repeat Steps 1 and 2 with the foundations for section c, making 6 rows as shown. Foundation piece, alternating black squares with tan rectangles.

Make 6.

I found it best to trim the seam allowances to ¼" and remove the paper before joining the center unit rows. If I caught even the tiniest bit of the paper, it really threw off these narrow strips—in this case, the paper was in my way, so I removed it.

4. Join the sections together in rows to complete the center unit.

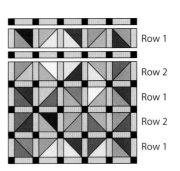

Row 1
Row 2
Row 1
Row 2
Row 1

SICILY BORDER

1. Trace or copy 46 section a foundations and 52 section b foundations from pattern pullout page P7. Set aside 4 section b's to use for border fillers.

2. Piece in numbered order.

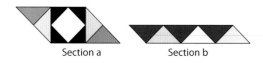

Section a   Section b

ote

Though section b foundations can be pieced in continuous strips, I suggest you make *several* long sections for each border. Chain sew and save time. Each section b foundation contains 6 triangles. You will need 48 complete foundations, and the remaining 4 can be cut apart as needed.

Tip

Glue sets of foundations together into continuous strips as shown for efficient chain sewing. When you cut the foundations from the paper, leave tabs at the ends. Put glue on each tab and overlap the adjacent foundation.

3. Join sections into rows as shown below. Press seams open between rows to distribute bulk. Working with diagonal foundations allows some seams to marry.

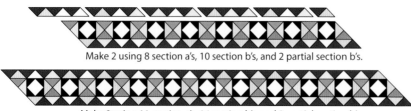

Make 2 using 8 section a's, 10 section b's, and 2 partial section b's.

Make 2 using 11 section a's, 14 section b's, and 2 partial section b's.

4. Copy and trace 4 foundations for the Sicily border fillers from pattern pullout page P6.

5. Piece sections c and d in numbered order. Sew section c to section d. Repeat to make 4 border fillers.

Filler unit

Make 4.

6. Add a border filler to each row. Note that you will attach the border filler to the same side of each border, so the border filler wraps around the corner.

Filler unit

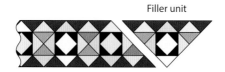

HERITAGE MEDALLION

1. Trace or copy the foundation from pattern pullout page P6.

2. Foundation piece the sections as shown in numbered order. Make 2 of each.

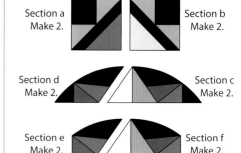

Section a
Make 2.

Section b
Make 2.

Section d
Make 2.

Section c
Make 2.

Section e
Make 2.

Section f
Make 2.

3. Join sections a and b in pairs; then join the pairs into a square. Join sections e and f to make 2 side sections. Join sections c and d to make the top and bottom sections. Add the side sections to the square and add the top and bottom sections to complete the medallion.

Section f   Section d
Section e   Section c

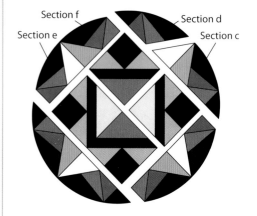

ELINOR MEDALLION

1. Trace or copy the foundation from pattern pullout page P5.

2. Foundation piece the sections in numbered order as shown. Make 4 each of sections b and c and 2 each of all the other sections.

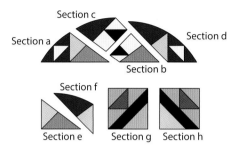

3. Join sections a, b, c, and d to make the top and bottom units. Join sections b, c, e, and f to make the side units. Join sections g and h to make the center square. Join the units as diagrammed to complete the medallion.

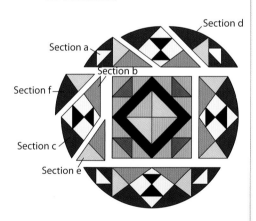

*N*ote

Remember that the color diagrams show the front of the unit, while the foundations are the back.

NORMAN MEDALLION

1. Trace or copy the foundation from pattern pullout page P7.

2. Foundation piece the sections in numbered order as shown. Make 4 of each section.

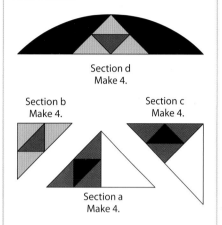

3. Join sections a and b. Sew sections together, alternating section a/b and section c. Stitch from the outside edge toward the center.

4. Refer to Doughnut Hole Appliqué (page 26), and iron a piece of freezer paper to the wrong side, covering the hole. Freezer paper is a useful "temporary fabric" for appliquéing the center circles to medallions.

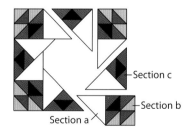

5. Make 2 circle templates from freezer paper, 4″ and 5½″ in diameter, respectively. Iron the larger circle to the wrong side of a beige scrap and the smaller circle to a taupe scrap. Cut out, adding a ¼″ seam allowance. Glue the seam allowance to the back of the template using a gluestick.

6. Machine appliqué the smaller circle to the larger, aligning the centers. After appliqué is complete, remove the papers, dampening the seam allowances with water to release the glue. Trim the seams to ¼″.

7. Appliqué the circles to the center of the medallion.

8. Add a section d to each side of the square to complete the medallion.

PALATINE MEDALLION

1. Trace or copy the foundation from pattern pullout page P8.

2. Foundation piece the sections as shown in numbered order. Make 8 of each section.

Section a
Make 8.

Section b
Make 8.

3. Join the pairs together to form a ring. *Do not trim off any of the excess seam allowance at the center.*

4. Make 2 circle templates from freezer paper, 7″ and 5½″ in diameter, respectively. Cut the larger circle from a taupe scrap and the smaller one from a gray scrap. Use the appliqué method described for the Norman medallion (page 83) to complete the design.

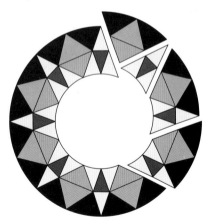

Curved Bands

Refer to Working with Curved Band Templates (page 24) for important information on how to make and use templates for the curved bands G.

1. Trace or copy 4 curved band foundations for each medallion from pullout pages P5–P8.

2. Join the quarters and press the seams open.

3. Mark the inside curve, and then tear the template to *keep the outside edge in place* but release the inside curve as shown on page 24.

4. Read the important instructions in Pinning and Sewing Curves (page 25). Sew the medallions into the circle bands. Press the seam toward the bands.

5. Glue the outside seam allowance to the back of the remaining edge of the freezer-paper template. This prepares the medallion for appliqué to the background.

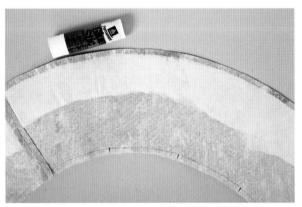

Background

1. Sew band A to the sides of the center unit.

2. Sew band B to the top and bottom.

3. Use the templates on pattern pullout page P4 to cut pieces for the background.

4. Join the background pieces to opposite sides of the pieced center unit.

5. Add the 2 background triangles to complete the rectangle.

6. Add band D to the sides and band C to the top and bottom of the background unit.

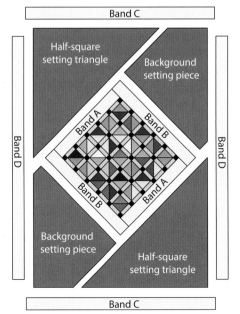

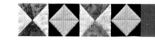

7. Position the medallions on the quilt top so they are barely touching the bands in the corners. *Allow them to overlap the center border.* There will be a slight space between the bands and the pieced center.

8. Use basting glue or pins to anchor the medallions in position. Machine appliqué with invisible thread, using a blind hem stitch or another stitch of your choice.

Borders

1. Sewing dot to dot, attach the border units to the top, bottom, and sides of the quilt. Join the corners with a diagonal Y-seam.

2. Add band E to each side and band F to the top and bottom to complete the quilt top.

DIAMANTE DELIGHT

Diamante Delight, 60″ × 92″, by Norah McMeeking, quilting by Kim Peterson of Kimberwood Quilting

Some Cosmati designers traveled far from Italy, and you can find examples of these as far away in time and space as Victorian England. The great crossing in Westminster Abbey is filled with a design credited to a thirteenth-century Roman, Odoricus, who came to London in 1268 to install it. My quilt is inspired by a portion of a floor in Bristol Cathedral, England, that was laid by Victorian restorers but no doubt inspired by the Cosmati.

This design uses "blocks" based on 60° equilateral triangles and diamonds. Take this opportunity to work with striking patterns that don't lend themselves to squares. Despite appearances, there are no set-in seams!

Before you begin, think about how you might vary this design:

- Fill the orange triangles with patchwork made up of half-units of diamonds.

- Put a compass in the center diamond or a pretty appliqué wreath.

- Simplify all the units by filling them with a grid of plain diamonds, like a slanted checkerboard.

Some 60° "block" designs are more easily interchanged than others. Alter the sample's blocks by adding more patches to existing designs or, conversely, eliminating smaller patches. Use the diamond patterns in the pullouts as the basis to redesign the "blocks." Though I encourage you to do your own thing with this design, the following describes how I made *Diamante Delight*.

Fabrics and Cutting Requirements

I used a mixed palette of approximately 5½ yards of varied prints, batiks, and solids in the patchwork areas of *Diamante Delight*. I chose brights, darks, light pastels, and grayed pastels in both prints and batiks.

Backing and binding: 6¼ yards

Batting: 68″ × 100″

HEXAGON STAR

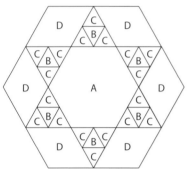

Piece in sections to make 9.

PATCH		FABRIC	CUTTING SIZE	TOTAL PATCHES
A	⬡	¼ yard medium pastels	4⅜″ strips	9
B	▱	¼ yard mixed dark scraps	2″ strips	66
C	▱	¼ yard mixed light scraps	2″ strips	198
D	▱60°	¼ yard mixed bright scraps	2½″ strips	40

DIAMOND PRISM

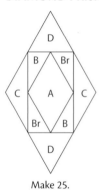

Make 25.

PATCH		FABRIC	CUTTING SIZE	TOTAL PATCHES
A	▱60°	¼ yard mixed scraps: half darks, half lights	2¾″ strips	25
B and Br	CT	⅜ yard mixed scraps: half darks, half lights	2½″ strips	100
C	CT	½ yard mixed scraps: half brights, half mediums	2″ strips	50
D	▱		2¾″ strips	50

*N*ote

Cut all hexagons and 60° diamonds and triangles from strips of the designated cutting width in the charts. See instructions in Cutting Other Shapes (page 17).

GLORIA'S STAR / GLORIOUS STAR

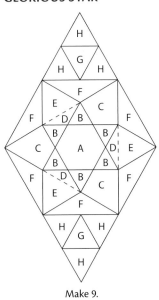

Make 9.

PATCH		FABRIC	CUTTING SIZE	TOTAL PATCHES
A	⬡	Mixed gold scraps	3" strips	9
B	▱	¼ yard mixed dark and medium scraps	2½" strips	27
C	CT	½ yard mixed light scraps	3½" strips	27
D	CT			27
E	▱			27
F	CT	⅝ yard mixed bright scraps	3" strips	54
G	▱	Mixed scraps	3" strips	18
H	▱	¼ yard mixed light scraps	3" strips	54

DIAMOND REFLECTIONS

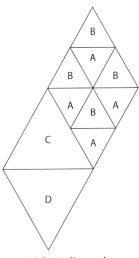

Make 25 diamonds.

PATCH		FABRIC	CUTTING SIZE	TOTAL PATCHES
A	▱	⅜ yard light scraps	3" strips	52
B	▱	⅜ yard dark scraps	3" strips	52
C	▱	⅛ yard light scraps	4½" strips	12
D	▱	⅛ yard mixed scraps	5" strips	12

TWISTING TRIANGLES

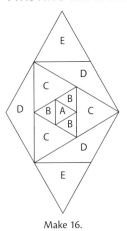

Make 16.

PATCH		FABRIC	CUTTING SIZE	TOTAL PATCHES
A	▱	Mixed red and gold scraps	2" strips	16
B	▱	⅛ yard mixed dark scraps	2" strips	48
C	▱	⅜ yard light scraps	3" strips	48
D	CT	½ yard mixed bright scraps	2" strips	48
E	▱	¼ yard mixed medium-light scraps	3½" strips	32

BANDS

BAND*	FABRIC	CUTTING SIZE	QUANTITY
A	2⅝ yards yellow batik	3″ × 21¾″	8
B		3″ × 71⅜″	2
C		3″ × 26⅝″	2
D		3″ × 78″	2
E		3″ × 50¼″	2

* Cut all bands on length of grain.

BORDERS

BORDER*	FABRIC	CUTTING SIZE	QUANTITY
Side	2⅜ yards brown batik	5½″ × 83″	2
Top/bottom		5½″ × 60¼″	2

* Cut border strips on length of grain.

SETTING TRIANGLES

FABRIC: 1⅜ yards pumpkin batik

The easiest way to cut these large triangles is to create freezer-paper templates. Use a sharp pencil and measure carefully. For non-freezer-paper templates, use pins. Draw the triangles as follows:

Triangles A and B

1. Draw a rectangle 19½″ × 33¾″ on freezer paper. Draw both diagonals. Triangle A is formed at the top and bottom, and triangle B is at the sides.

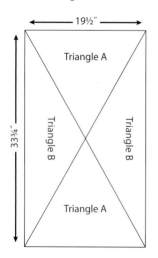

2. Cut out the freezer-paper triangles. Press them to the background fabric, leaving room for seam allowances. Cut, *adding ¼″ seam allowances* on all sides.

Triangles C and Cr

1. Draw 2 rectangles 9¾″ × 16⅞″ on freezer paper. Draw the diagonals—either diagonal will do because you need triangle C and its reverse.

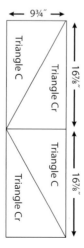

2. Cut out the freezer-paper triangles. Press the triangles to the back of a piece of fabric, leaving room for seam allowances. Cut, *adding a ¼″ seam allowance* on all sides.

Tip

If your freezer paper isn't wide enough, cut a length the extra width you need plus 2″. Lay the paper same side up, with edges overlapping, side by side. Use a machine basting stitch to sew the two pieces together—overlap, not a proper seam!

This holds the sheets together better than glue, tape, or ironing.

Important: Add a ¼″ seam allowance to the outside of the triangle templates as you cut out the fabric. Alternatively, make separate drawings for each triangle and add a ¼″ seam allowance to the outside of all the triangles to make cutting-size templates.

Paper Foundations

Read General Instructions (pages 17–27) before starting.

Note

CAUTION

Remember that stitching lines are on what will be the *wrong side* of the completed block. Keep that reversal in mind when color placement varies or blocks have a direction (such as the Diamond Reflections block).

Foundation Piecing

HEXAGON STAR

1. Trace or copy 21 section a foundations, 9 section b foundations, 17 section c foundations, 15 section d foundations, and 4 section e foundations from pattern pullout page P6.

2. Piece in numbered order.

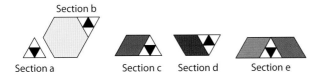

3. Assemble the sections into rows.

Make 4 rows.

Make 3 rows.

4. Sew the rows together in the order shown.

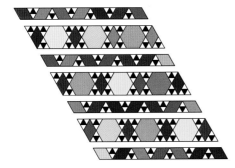

DIAMOND PRISM

1. Trace or copy 25 foundations from pattern pullout page P6.

2. Piece in numbered order.

3. Trim the seam allowance to ¼″ using the edges of the foundations as a guide. Carefully remove the papers.

4. Sew the blocks into rows.

5. Join the rows.

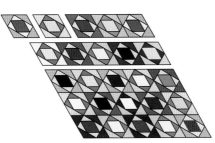

GLORIA'S STAR

1. Trace or copy 9 foundations from pattern pullout page P8.

2. Piece each section in numbered order.

*N*ote

Patches 1b, 3b, 6c, 6d, and 2e *must be the same fabric* because they form the background for the star.

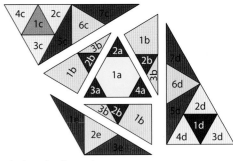

Block made of 7 sections

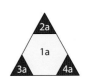

Section a: Make 9.

Section b: Make 27.

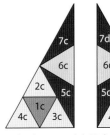

Sections c and d: Make 9 of each.

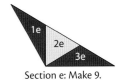

Section e: Make 9.

3. Join a section b to each side of section a.

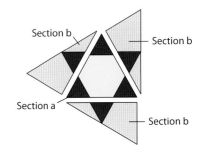

Section b · Section b · Section a · Section b

4. Add section c, then section d, and finally section e to complete the block. Press the seams open.

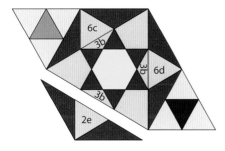

5. Join 3 blocks to make a row. Join in diagonal rows.

DIAMOND REFLECTIONS

Note

Tick marks are included on the foundation in case you wish to vary the design.

1. Trace or copy 13 full foundations from pattern pullout page P8. Cut 10 apart to separate sections a and b. Cut the remaining 3 foundations into a total of 12 large triangles.

2. Piece in numbered order.

Note

The foundations are the same, but the value placement varies.

Light/bright: Make 10. Dark/light: Make 10. Dark: Make 3. Light: Make 3. Bright: Make 2. Light: Make 2.

3. Arrange the diamonds into rows; make 3 of Row 1 and 2 of Row 2.

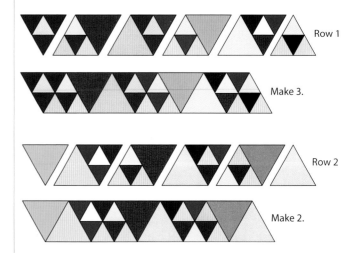

Row 1

Make 3.

Row 2

Make 2.

4. Join the rows, alternating Rows 1 and 2 to complete the unit.

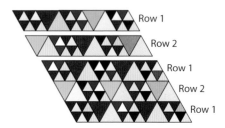

Row 1
Row 2
Row 1
Row 2
Row 1

TWISTING TRIANGLES

1. Trace or copy 16 foundations from pattern pullout page P8.

2. Piece in numbered order.

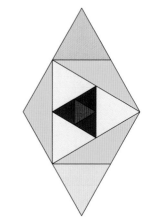

Remember the fabric side of the block is the reverse of the foundation.

3. Join the blocks together into rows of 4. The seams will marry if you rotate every other block. Join the rows together to complete the unit.

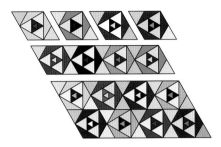

Quilt Assembly

Trim the corners of bands A, B, and C. Work with the fabric right side up in Steps 1–3 to trim the corner angles by 30° or 60°, using the angles marked on a quilter's ruler. Align the edge of the band with the correct line on the ruler and trim off excess fabric. Mark the dots if you wish.

Tip

Consider marking the angle on each band with a washout pen and put in position to double check before actually trimming!

1. Trim all bands A with 60° angles at both ends, as shown.

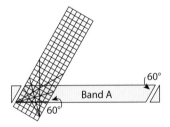

2. Trim both bands B, with 60° and 30° angles, as shown.

Line up the ruler with the edge of the band carefully, right into the corner angle, and trim.

3. Trim both bands C with 60° and 30° angles, as shown.

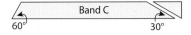

4. Sew a band A to the top and bottom edges of each section except Gloria's Star, matching the angled ends.

5. Sew Gloria's Star between Hexagon Star and Twisting Triangles.

6. Sew band B to each side of that unit.

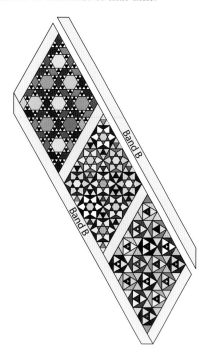

7. Sew a band C to the edge of the Diamond Reflections unit and to the Diamond Prism unit. If you trimmed them correctly, they will fit only the intended side of the unit.

8. Add setting triangles A and B to the units as shown.

9. Add corner setting triangles C and Cr to each corner.

10. Sew the diagonal rows together as shown.

11. Sew band D to each side and band E to the top and bottom of the quilt.

12. Finish by adding the side borders and then the top and bottom borders to complete the quilt.

Norah McMeeking worked as a graphic designer before trading in her T-square for a Pfaff. She loves designing and teaching—anything! Because she's married to a professor of engineering, she has ample time to sew as well as the opportunity to travel with his air miles. Norah admires all forms and fashions of quiltmaking. A true people person, she enjoys encouraging her students to do their own thing and relishes the time she spends with quilters. She exhibits her quilts and has won awards both nationally and internationally. She serves as a juror and judge for exhibits whenever possible. Norah makes her home (and a mess) in Santa Barbara, California.

Photo by Jon Conyers

Top row: Norah McMeeking, Karin Cooper, Barbara Aspen; *Center row:* Irelle Beatie, Adela LaBand, Ky Easton, Jeanne Morrison Phillips; *Front row:* Mary Ballard, Jan Inouye, Julie Cohen; *Not pictured:* Isabel Bartholome, Colby Kline, Sandy Wilmot

RESOURCES

Contact the author

Norah is happy to answer questions at www.bellabellaquilts.com

Machine Quilters and Piecers

QUILTING DESIGNERS

Dee Angus, Tomorrow's Treasures, Ojai, California
angus@west.net   805-559-4582

Kimberly Peterson, Kimberwood Quilting, Lindon, Utah
www.kimberwoodquilting.com
kim@peterzone.org

Paula Rostkowski, A Quilter's Work, Grayslake, Illinois
www.aquilterswork.com
paula@aquilterswork.com

THE BELLA BRIGADE

Talented quilters from the Santa Barbara area in California lent their time and enthusiasm to the creation of many of the quilts in this book. Their generosity is much appreciated by the author, who couldn't have managed without them.

Previous books by author

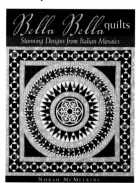

Great Titles and Products

from C&T PUBLISHING

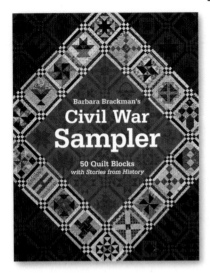

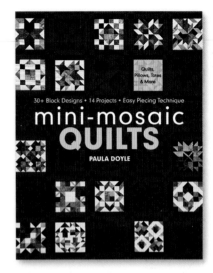

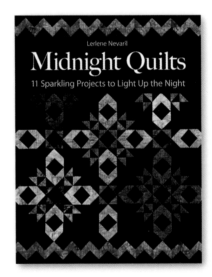

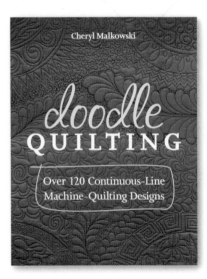

Available at your local retailer or **www.ctpub.com** *or* **800-284-1114**

For a list of other fine books from C&T Publishing, visit our website to view our catalog online.

C&T PUBLISHING, INC.
P.O. Box 1456
Lafayette, CA 94549
800-284-1114

Email: ctinfo@ctpub.com
Website: www.ctpub.com

C&T Publishing's professional photography services are now available to the public. Visit us at www.ctmediaservices.com.

Tips and Techniques can be found at www.ctpub.com > Consumer Resources > Quiltmaking Basics: Tips & Techniques for Quiltmaking & More

For quilting supplies:

COTTON PATCH
1025 Brown Ave.
Lafayette, CA 94549
Store: 925-284-1177
Mail order: 925-283-7883

Email: CottonPa@aol.com
Website: www.quiltusa.com

Note: Fabrics shown may not be currently available, as fabric manufacturers keep most fabrics in print for only a short time.